saving amy

saving amy

daphne barak

NEW
HOLLAND

Published in 2010 by New Holland Publishers (UK) Ltd
London • Cape Town • Sydney • Auckland
www.newhollandpublishers.com
Garfield House, 86–88 Edgware Road, London W2 2EA, United Kingdom
80 McKenzie Street, Cape Town 8001, South Africa
Unit 1, 66 Gibbes Street, Chatswood, NSW 2067, Australia
218 Lake Road, Northcote, Auckland, New Zealand

10 9 8 7 6 5 4 3 2 1

A catalogue record for this book is available from the British Library

ISBN 978 1 84773 670 3

Publishing Director: Rosemary Wilkinson
Publisher: Aruna Vasudevan
Project Editor: Julia Shone
Cover Design: Cabin London Ltd
Inside Design: Rebecca Longworth Book Design
Production: Melanie Dowland

Reproduction by Pica Digital Pte Ltd, Singapore
Printed in the UK by CPI William Clowes, Beccles, NR34 7TL

The paper used to produce this book is sourced from sustainable forests.

daphne barak

Daphne Barak is one of the few leading A-list interviewers in the world who conducts a wide range of sit-down television interviews with celebrities, heads-of-state, royals, Hollywood stars and musicians. Her exclusives and television specials air and are printed in the leading outlets, in their own languages, in many countries around the world, including USA, UK, Germany, France, Italy, Spain, Portugal, Netherlands, Switzerland, Ireland, Croatia, Russia, Greece, Bulgaria, Turkey, Arab world, Pakistan, India, Far East, Brazil, Australia and New Zealand.

Daphne owns her library, which consists of more than 200 filmed interviews, including Obama and Clinton specials, exclusives with Pakistani leaders, Saddam Hussein, Fidel Castro, Mike Tyson, Muammar al-Qaddafi, Robert Mugabe, Nelson Mandela, O.J. Simpson, Mother Teresa, Yasser Arafat, Shimon Peres, Benazir Bhutto, Eric Clapton, Lindsay England, Lisa Minnelli, Mia Farrow, Robert De Niro, Johnny Depp and Michael Jackson.

Daphne spends a lot of time with her interviewees, uncovering the issues in-depth and ensuring that a whole new picture comes alive with each exclusive.

This book is dedicated to Ehud Barak,
Miriam Barak and Dov Barak.

contents

preface

'*...Sounds Afro-American: is British-Jewish. Looks sexy: won't play up to it. Is young: sounds old. Sings sophisticated: talks rough. Musically mellow: lyrically nasty.*' This is the paradox that is Amy Winehouse, according to music journalist Garry Mulholland.

What else? *...Award-winning musician. Flamboyant pop star. Style icon. The new Brigitte Bardot. A once-pocket Venus. Drug addict. Alcoholic....* The list of words used to describe the phenomenon that is 'Amy Winehouse' is, it seems, endless.

Arguably, one of the greatest and certainly most original talents to emerge in the 21st century, Amy fascinates us all. Her life is one endless soap opera – if you believe the paparazzi. Her thoughts on everything from the weakness of an ex-boyfriend to how she feels about her Dad and his infidelity are immortalized in her music (in the songs 'Stronger Than Me' and 'What Is It About Men' respectively, which are both included on Amy's 2003 debut album, *Frank*) for everyone to hear. And, she doesn't appear to care.

preface

Since she first came into most people's music consciousness after the release of the critically acclaimed, platinum-selling album *Frank* (2003), mostly about that same ex-boyfriend, followed by the Grammy-winning *Back To Black* (2006), Amy Winehouse has seldom been out of the news.

Her turbulent on-again, off-again relationship with former husband Blake Fielder-Civil, her dramatic performances on- and off-stage and her relationship with her father, Mitch, or mother, Janis, grab headlines around the world. And, everyone loves to read about Amy. Everyone certainly has an opinion about her – her music, her marriage, her behaviour, her addictions, her hair.... Everyone knows 'Amy'.

...Or, perhaps that's what she lets them *think*.

☆ ☆ ☆

The idea for *Saving Amy* arose in 2008, when Mitch Winehouse first asked to meet me in London. At that point, Amy Winehouse was in the news, less for her talent and more for her alleged addictions, erratic behaviour, hospitalizations and her relationship with Blake.

We met, a couple of times, at *Les Ambassadeurs*, an exclusive private member's club in Mayfair, where Mitch impressed me by seemingly talking frankly about his daughter. He wasn't defensive and he didn't appear to take offence at any of my questions.

At our second meeting at the club, in November 2008, when Mitch was actually beginning to convince me that this might be an interesting project and that we should start filming, he said something that caught my attention, something which I immediately understood.

'Daphne, at the end of the day, I'm going to talk only once about my private life – my family's private life – do you understand?'

Well, of course, I understood. Who wants to share his private life, his *family's* private life, especially a complicated one, more than once? Once is usually hard enough.

During the course of that meeting, we discussed making a documentary film, one that should be from Mitch's viewpoint, to show how addiction not only affects the person who is afflicted but also how it impacts on his or her immediate family, extended family, friends, and so on.

At one point, after I had asked Mitch how this talented and charismatic young woman had reached this point, he gestured to the photograph that he had been clutching throughout our meeting. It showed a young, beautiful, big-eyed Amy Winehouse, brimming with confidence. Staring at it, Mitch told me that Amy had been holed up in London, in bed, hiding under the covers, for weeks now.

Suddenly Mitch's mobile rang. His face immediately lit up.

'It's Amy!', he exclaimed.

He chatted with his daughter briefly before hanging up.

A short while later, his phone rang again, and it was Amy. Mitch was obviously pleased, but for the rest of our meeting, I noticed that he periodically glanced at his phone nervously, almost willing it to ring again.

He finally admitted to me: 'I am worried when I get a phone call from her or her security [people] because I don't know what bad news I may get. But when I

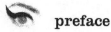

preface

don't hear from her or her security, I am worried as well – what might have happened [sic]?'

Then, Mitch said the words that cemented my decision to make the film: 'When Amy's addiction began, I went to private doctors, to experts, to learn about the problem. I had no knowledge, nobody to talk to. You feel so helpless, yet we can afford, financially, more than other people who face the same problem. So if I can share what I have gone through, and what I have learned, and by doing so help at least one other family … then this is what I would like to do.'

That's how it all began…

☆ ☆ ☆

My meetings with the Winehouses over the next few months, in London, Switzerland and St Lucia, are certainly never dull and I learn a lot about their relationships with each other and their daughter through our conversations, their interaction with each other and my own observations of them – and this book is the result of that time.

Saving Amy is based not just on the taped interviews, but also on my diaries and personal notes and recollections while spending time with Mitch, Janis, Jane (Mitch's wife) and Amy, herself.

This book is certainly not meant to be a biography, but it is an exploration of addiction. Through the words and first-hand experiences of those closest to Amy Winehouse, my aim is to show the love, fear and powerlessness, indeed, the emotions that most families experience as they watch firsthand the spiralling out of control of their loved ones. In this case, the subject may be a young woman who is certainly one of the most talented musicians of her generation, but having a talent doesn't make addiction any easier to live with.

The one constant throughout our discussions is the love that Mitch and Janis have, and often express, for Amy. But my interviews and meetings with the Winehouse family, and, indeed, with the many other people who I have interviewed over the years and who have discussed addictions with me (and these include Eric Clapton, Michael Jackson, Liza Minnelli, Kathleen Turner, Barry Manilow, Kid Rock, Art Garfunkel, Michael Bolton, Charlton Heston, Donatella Versace, Roberto Cavalli and Omar Sharif), have raised many questions with me about the nature of addiction and how it is caused.

While, without a doubt, Amy Winehouse is loved, is that love healthy? How much of her addiction is fuelled by something in her past? How much stems from the relationship that Amy not only has with her father, but with others, such as those existing between Mitch and Janis, Mitch and Jane, Jane and Janis, and Mitch with all three of the women in his life?

Similarly, is it possible that families sometimes fuel the addictions of their loved ones, admittedly without necessarily knowing that they're doing so? And, what can be done to break this cycle, when it does happen?

These are just some of the questions I had to ask myself both during filming and also off camera when I spoke to these people individually and watched how they interacted with each other and with Amy, herself. Now, for me, one question, out of all of them, stands out: Just what happened to Amy Winehouse in the past to make her want to pursue the path which she is currently following?

will you still love me tomorrow?

In any story, whether a film or a book, the usual place to start is at the beginning. So, when we start filming *Saving Amy* in November 2008, it seems right to go back to the place where Mitch Winehouse and his first wife, Janis, grew up – in London's East End.

Much has been made about Amy Winehouse's 'normal' family upbringing, the North London Jewish community in which both she and her parents grew up and the influence that her grandmother Cynthia, Mitch's mother, in particular, had on the young Amy. Family plays a big part in Amy's life, as becomes increasingly evident in the discussions that I have over the next months with the Winehouses and, later, Amy herself.

Amy's family has shaped the way in which she's grown up, the decisions she's made – even the kind of musician she's become – and this place, where Amy's parents grew up, is an integral part of all that, of helping to explain how Amy has become the person she is today.

Mitch, accompanied by my film crew and I in my two limousines, drive around the places where he grew up as a child.

'This is Albert Gardens[1],' he tells our chauffeur. 'And this is the place where I grew up and where my Mum grew up. As you can see, even now it is very attractive. It was actually built for sea captains, so I was told; I don't know if it is true or not. It is a nice place.'

Mitch lived here when he was younger and went to school in Stepney, about half a mile from where we're currently sitting. The whole of this part of London is rich in culture and history, a place where Jack the Ripper walked the streets, where immigrants first settled when they came to England, where local Jews, Irish dockers and Oswald Mosley's black shirts came to blows, as Mitch tells us, on Mansell Street, in what became known as the Battle of Cable Street[2].

'There was no racial tension,' Mitch says, 'or anything that I can remember as a child – not in this area.'

It's obvious that Mitch loves this place. With great pride, he points out the maternity hospital where his mother and her twin sister, Lorna, were born, and talks about the cinema that used to be there, the Troxy-Gaumont. That picture house and one in Mile End formed a big part of his life growing up: it was in these places that his grandmother, 'Bubba', could be found most days, and which formed a microcosm of life in the East End.

'I can tell you some stories,' he reminisces. '... You couldn't watch the film because people were eating, they were chewing, they were laughing, they were making love. It was fantastic. It was great times. When you look at it now, it is still nice, isn't it?'

When I ask Mitch to tell me a bit about his mother, Cynthia, and the effect she had on him and on Amy, he comments emotionally: '… A lot has been written about my mum and her influence on Amy, and of course this place [Albert Gardens] had the greatest influence on my mother and on me because this is where we both grew up and you can see even today what a lovely place it is….

'I think a place; your upbringing has got a lot to do with your character.' He adds, 'I still love it here: it's funny isn't it? It is like my home.'

When Mitch was a child, he lived at 31, Albert Gardens. And, it's here we end up. His grandmother lived in the house from the early 1920s until her death.

When we arrive there, we walk along Albert Gardens. Mitch comments that every house here was Jewish when he was growing up.

'There are still a few old Jews here today,' he adds.

'This is the house,' he says, stopping outside one of the buildings. 'The same front door. There used to be a board there, because they were dressmakers so they would put a board and the board would say they need a felling hand, which was someone who pressed. They would need a presser and the vacancies would be up there. That was our lounge down there. That was our front room.' He points to various rooms as he speaks.

I have to admit I'm quite surprised at the size of the building. It's big, maybe three or four storeys high. I say this to Mitch.

'Yeah,' he comments. 'It was big inside.'

I ask him to tell me who lived there with him when he was growing up and he reels off several names – his mother, Cynthia, her twin, Lorna, who shared the first floor room, also his grandmother, his great uncle, and on the top floor, a man named Izzy Hammer, who was a holocaust survivor – they all lived in the house.

'This place has really great memories,' Mitch says. 'And Amy and my son, Alex, they love coming here, although obviously my grandmother had gone by the time they came along.'

☆ ☆ ☆

Janis and Mitch first met through Martin, Janis's cousin, who was Mitch's best friend from the age of 13. Janis was just eight or nine when the boys became friends and Mitch thought she was horrible then. They didn't really meet again until 1975, when Janis was about 22 or 23 and a pharmacy technician; by then, Mitch was a double-glazing salesman.

'And all of a sudden this horrible little eight-year-old was now a beautiful young woman,' Mitch reminisces. 'And I pestered Martin for a year or two to make the introduction, but he wisely thought I wasn't good enough for his cousin, but somehow we got together ...'.

Things actually took off between Mitch and Janis after they bumped into each other at a party. Hilary, Mitch's girlfriend at the time, went off with someone else and Janis and Mitch ended up spending the evening together.

'The rest, as they say, is history,' Mitch murmurs.

I get an opportunity to ask Janis about that day when I interview her with Mitch later in November 2008. Mitch had originally told me that it might be a problem speaking to Janis. She suffers from multiple sclerosis (MS) and she walks with a cane. When Mitch describes Janis, he says she is disabled. Mitch is obviously mystified, when Janis agrees to see me: 'I don't understand why she agreed so fast,' he says.

I like Janis immensely and when we put her and Mitch together, there is no doubt that she steals the show.

When did they meet? I ask Janis. At a party on 11 October 1975, she replies; Mitch counters that he thought that it was November.

Janis continues, 'I'd just come back from America and it was a case of Mitchell asking me to dance. And I knew at that moment that "yes" would mean life. I knew we would be together, the whole time, and it was a case of "yes" or "no", so I said "yes!"'

'And we were married two hours later!' Mitch interjects. 'No! That's not true.'

Janis initially kept the fact that she was going out with Mitch a secret from friends and family, even though Mitch had given her a ring by that stage. She comments, '... If everyone knew I was with Mitch they'd go: "Oh no! No! No!"'

Mitch seems surprised by this and asks his ex-wife why she says that. She explains: 'Because you were like rowdy and it was a case of, like, are you mad? So, I kept to myself ... it was a secret that I was going out with Mitchell.'

Janis always refers to her ex-husband as Mitchell during our conversations.

'She was ashamed!' Mitch comments, laughing.

Janis just says, 'It was a case of people would say "Why?! WHY?!"'

I ask them if it was love at first sight for both of them. Mitch says that it's hard to explain how it works, but adds that he just knew that it was right. Even so, the road to marriage wasn't plain sailing for them by any means. As Mitch says, 'We had a few ups and downs. Janis was very good with money and I wasn't so she had to discipline me on a number of occasions. ... Actually she called our engagement off.'

He continues, 'I felt so ill, I couldn't go to work. I begged her to come out with me for the day. I thought, "I've got to do something to make it up", so I phoned in and said my grandmother had passed away. And, it's what happened that day. My grandmother passed away. On that day ... You've gotta be careful what you wish for ...'.

'My grandmother passed away,' he repeats, 'but Janis and I were still together. That was the summer of '75 or '76. Then, we got married in December of that year.'

But not everyone was happy about it. Janis's mother thought her daughter would marry a professional. Mitch says when his mother found out what Janis's mother had said, she 'wiped the floor with her.'

'I was a professional,' Mitch protests. 'A professional croupier!', but adds that Janis's mother never really came to terms with their relationship.

Janis and Mitch settled down to married life in a small two-bedroom flat in Southgate in North London and the heart of the Jewish community. In 1979, their son, Alex, was born, followed four years later, on 14 September 1983 by Amy.

In one of our early interviews, Mitch described Amy's birth at Chase Farm Hospital in Enfield, commenting that his daughter has always been in a hurry and her birth seemed to be no different.

'… That particular night she was in a hurry because my ex-wife Janis had been taking – I think it's called extract of raspberry to help her with the birth because when my son was born she found it quite traumatic, and she was advised this extract of raspberry or strawberry, something like that, would help with the birth, so Janis went into labour and literally 10 minutes later Amy was born. It was possibly the quickest labour in the world and they had to catch her; she nearly fell off the table. She flew out literally, so – now we joke, she was in a hurry to get out and she's always in a rush.'

Janis says, '… She was four days late.'

'Was she? I don't remember that. I think she and Alex were both four days late!'

Janis says that she thought Amy would be another boy, like Alex. 'I thought, I don't know what to do with a girl. I knew what to do with a boy, changing nappies and everything. I didn't know what to do with a girl! And then she arrived and she looked just like her brother did. Exactly! Same baby, yeah!'

Both Mitch and Janis have commented in many interviews on how beautiful Amy was. Amy was a lovely baby, Mitch agrees, and did indeed look like her brother, Alex. She now, Mitch insists, looks the spitting image of Janis. 'She has her hair short and if I showed you a picture of Janis when she was 25 you can barely tell the difference. They are very much alike.'

This is still true. It strikes me when I finally meet Janis with my film crew at the Hotel Intercontinental in London. My first thoughts are: 'Here comes Amy. She is *so* Amy – before the heavy drugs and alcohol kick in.'

☆ ☆ ☆

When you have a daughter who is as famous as Amy Winehouse, a singer renowned for her unique voice and brilliance as a musician, you would think that there must have been some indication of that talent early on in her childhood. Or was there? I ask Mitch and Janis about this.

'She always loved music,' Mitch says. 'We were a family that sang and danced.'

Certainly music is in both Mitch and Janis's backgrounds. Mitch's mother, Cynthia, who Amy was really close to, was once engaged to the legendary jazz saxophonist Ronnie Scott, and her uncle Leon was a professional horn player. Amy grew up in a house full of music – Janis listening to Carole King and James Taylor, Mitch listening to the artists he now covers when he performs live, as he shows me later at his club in Chiswick, West London. 'Jazz, Sinatra, whatever my voice can handle. It's enjoyable,' he says.

Mitch is a surprisingly entertaining performer – he has a pleasant voice and you can see that he loves to be in the limelight. Of course, there's a big difference between having a good voice and being an artist – Amy expresses her pain, love and even her addictions in her songs and this is something that Mitch cannot compete with. He can never steal the show from Amy completely, but there's no doubt that he enjoys the attention.

I ask Mitch when the first time was that he thought, 'My God, my baby can sing?'

'There was no real indication, apart from the fact that we were always singing, there was no indication as a child or a baby ... she was very clever as a small child, very manipulative. She would know how to pull everyone's chain. She knew how to in a nice way, not a bad way,' Mitch adds.

That's *every* girl, I comment.

Mitch continues, '... She was quite clever, and she knew how to kind of manipulate people. But in a nice way,' he repeats.

He talks about the first time he can really remember Amy performing, at probably 15 or 16 months old. 'I would sing to her, even before she spoke. I would sing a little song and I would leave a word out and she would fill the word in, so I would sing –'

'Can you sing it?' I interrupt.

'I used to sing, you know that song ... "*Are the stars out tonight, I don't know if it's cloudy or bright, for I only have eyes for* ..." and she would go "*You!*" And I would sing another line and she would fill in a little word. She was very cute!

'... She was kind of talking and singing at the same time. As she got bigger, maybe two, we would stand her on the table and she would sing a little song. My son [Alex] would sing too.'

'Your son sings as well?' I ask, interested to hear something about Alex.

'No, he's not a good singer.' Mitch replies. 'You know, as a child he would sing.'

'... [But] I have been taking him to Spurs since he was two.' Alex is more into football, it seems.

Mitch tells me that Amy also used to be keen on ice skating and Mitch took her to Alexandra Palace in North London. 'She was a very good ice skater and I remember the first time I took her, I couldn't believe it. She was messing about and she was really good.'

☆ ☆ ☆

After Amy was born, the family moved to a 1930s semi-detached house, also in Southgate. Both of Jewish ancestry, Mitch and Janis made sure that their children were culturally aware. Amy attended cheder classes[3] every Saturday, and as a family, the Winehouses went to the synagogue on Yom Kippur, but for Amy, being Jewish was all about being together as a real family.

When Amy was four years old, she went to Osidge Primary School in North London, which has a strong music focus. It was there that she began to show a real interest in performing. Pretending to be Pepsi & Shirley, the backing singers of 1980s pop band Wham!, Amy sang with her friend Juliette Ashby, who Amy later wrote about in her song 'Best Friends'. Speaking to the *Observer* about that friendship, Amy said, 'I think we clicked because we were both a bit off-key.'

Off-key or not, Amy sang all the time, Janis recalls.

'Well, you'd remember that more than me,' Mitch comments.

'... Amy would sing, all the time, all the time, and whatever she was doing she'd sing and Alex and myself,'

Janis recalls, 'would say, "Shut up, Amy!" She just would never stop singing.'

'I don't remember that,' Mitch murmurs.

I ask Janis what Amy used to sing.

'Whatever the current record of the moment was. … Or Mitchell would sing a song and Amy would imitate him.'

I ask Janis if she can sing. She immediately recounts a story about Amy being asked that very question on a radio show. Amy said she'd originally thought everyone in the family could sing because she could and her Dad could. 'But then she said, "I heard my Mum sing and I realized that not *everyone* could …!"'

Amy was about eight or nine years old when Janis really started to realize that her daughter had something special. Amy, Janis and her mother-in-law, Cynthia, who Janis thought of more as a mother, went to Cyprus together. Amy took part in a cabaret with some other children. 'Somebody there said, "Oh! Have you got a manager? You know she [Amy] could be really professional" and we were like, "No, no, no!" and we just pushed it away.'

The family also had other things to deal with at the time. When Amy was nine years old, Mitch and Janis separated. Mitch had been openly involved for a very long time with another woman, Jane, who went on to become his second wife.

☆ ☆ ☆

In an interview in 2007, Janis spoke about the break-up. 'We'd had a very agreeable marriage but he was never there. He was a salesman so he was away a lot, but for a long time there was also another woman, Jane, who became his second wife. I think Mitchell would have liked to have both of us but I wasn't happy to do that.'

I witnessed this firsthand at the party I threw for Mitch in late December at *Les Ambassadeurs* club, in London. Flanked by his beautifully turned out first and second wives, Janis and Jane, Mitch made his strong but perhaps ambivalent feelings for them known when he said, '… Somehow I managed to find this woman [gesturing to Janis], first of all, and this lovely lady [Jane], after that. And, erm, it's their misfortune, I understand, but I'm the lucky one. They're not so lucky. I'm the lucky one and this is what it's all about. … Okay, these women are just fantastic. They are strong women, Janis and Jane. I love them both – only Jane just a little bit more. So, that's the way that it goes.'

Their parent's breakup was tough for both Amy and Alex. As Mitch commented in one of our first interviews together, they were always a loving family. 'There's lot of kisses and cuddles. Lots of telling stories before they [went] to bed and things like that. Just a normal, perfectly normal, loving family.'

And, of course, this dynamic had to change after the divorce when Jane replaced their mother as Mitch's wife.

I tell Mitch, 'I know you are very close [to Amy], that is why we are here. There is no good recipe to be a good parent. And every parent questions himself or herself and says, "Did I do the right thing?"'

He comments, '… I have looked back and thought how could we have done things differently. Maybe if I had stayed with Amy's Mum. I am not saying I was unhappy with Amy's Mum. I wanted to be with Jane. What would that have done to me? Maybe that would have made the situation worse. Maybe if I had been firmer with her [Amy]. Maybe I was too firm with her.

'It is difficult to look back through the course of time as to one's parenting skills. We always did the best that we could. Our children were always the most important things for us. They weren't an appendage. They weren't a possession. They were our little friends. They were there to be helped and cherished and nourished and looked after, and we did the best that we could.

'We *really* did the best that we could and we encouraged them and we didn't bully them and we didn't hit them. We did the best that we could in our own limited way without going on a course in how to be the best parents in the world. We did really the best that we could. Maybe we could have done better, I don't know.'

I ask Mitch about his relationship with Janis after the divorce. '[We] get on great. What is even nicer is that Janis and my wife, Jane, get on very well. … My wife is a nice person. My ex-wife is a nice person and I like to think that I am a nice person.'

I have to wonder, at this point, if Mitch really understands the dynamic that exists between Janis and Jane. In fact, Janis told me, on one occasion, that one of the hardest things for her to face, when Amy was in hospital in November 2008, was the fact that Jane, the woman that Mitch left her for, was sitting on the other side of her daughter's bed. It seems that for Janis there is still a lot of pain attached to her divorce from Mitch and so his claim that everyone gets on well doesn't really ring true. Perhaps it's just easier for him to think that.

During the interviews, Mitch looks guilty when the matter of his divorce comes up. He often seems to torment himself, questioning whether his behaviour has led to Amy's troubles and addictions. He tells me, '… The problem was that when we split up, I tried to overindulge the children a little bit too much. … I had a manufacturing company [then]. We had 400 employees. … I would work early in the morning before the children got up. … I came to the house. I got them ready for school. I took them to school. … I came back from work to pick them up from school. … I wouldn't leave them alone. I wanted to be with them all the time. … I was at the house all the time and Janis had to say to me, "We are divorced; you really aren't meant to be here." In a nice way. We were trying to get over the fact that we were divorced, which was difficult for her more than me because I had Jane and it wasn't appropriate for me to be there all the time.'

Mitch, at one point during our early interviews, says that Amy's brother, Alex, suffered from depression for three years. He adds, 'Looking back Amy wasn't affected because she knew Jane from when Amy was two. She has known Jane her whole life. Alex knew Jane from when he was six. I thought it was Alex who was more affected by our break-up but clearly Alex has got over it. Alex is fine. … When we split up, Alex was older.'

When I first meet Janis in London, I get the chance to ask if she thinks Amy's troubles began with her divorce from Mitch. 'No, no, no,' she denies. 'I am very much a person of – it was life's experience – and that's it. We go through life and we experience it in our way.'

Yet, when I am with Amy in St Lucia months later, it occurs to me that, while there might not be a rift between

Janis and Mitch, Amy still behaves like that 9-year-old kid, trying to grab her parents' attention. She needs it – craves it.

I ask Janis what her wish was for Amy and Alex when they were growing up. 'For them to be happy and do what is best for them. And, that's all I wanted for them. And they are both, both very, very talented. They are probably equally talented.'

Janis continues: 'Mitchell and I always joke about Alex and Amy and Mitchell would always say "Alex, we adopted you" and Alex would be like "What! What! What! What!" – because that was the joke on them. And it would always be that either Alex was adopted or Amy was adopted. Just to throw them off-key.'

On the occasions that Janis and I meet or speak over the next months, it occurs to me that she continually drops 'Mitchell and I' into the conversation, in the way you would do if you were a couple. Although Janis is a woman who was abandoned by her husband and the father of her two children for another woman (about whom Janis had known for quite some time, as had Amy and Alex, from the ages of two and six respectively), in her mind she and Mitch are still a couple, still united.

When it comes to Amy, Jane is only the other woman and can't compete. Janis and Mitch are Amy's parents – Jane simply doesn't enter into the equation.

☆ ☆ ☆

After Janis and Mitch split up, Janis moved with Alex and Amy to a house in East Finchley, another Jewish-dominated area in North London. Amy is reported to have said that growing up there was 'cool', but it must have been very different to the life that she and her brother had had until then.

Janis recalls that Amy missed Mitch not being around and that this might be why there is a lot of anger in her songs. Mitch's treatment of Janis and his affair with Jane is certainly something Amy deals with in her song 'What Is It About Men'.

Aged 11, Amy moved to Ashmole Secondary School in Southgate, along with her friend, Juliette, where her musical tastes began to change and broaden. She listened to jazz, the music that Mitch liked so much and her uncles played, and sang along to artists like Ella Fitzgerald and Sarah Vaughan, a singer who inspired Amy to realize that a 'whisper can be so much more effective than just belting something out.'

Amy performed in amateur youth plays and school productions, sometimes more successfully than others, as Mitch noted in an early discussion. Recalling when he and Jane went to see a 12-year-old Amy sing at school, he commented, 'She sang this song ... and I said to Jane "Well, thank God she can have a career as an actress." And the next year she [Amy] said, "Dad I am in this concert, will you come and see us?" So I said to my wife, "Well, we have got to go." So, we went to see her and in a space of a year she could already sing. I remember the song she sang ... the Alanis Morissette "Isn't It Ironic" and it was great, so now in the space of a year she could sing. Whether it was in the right key I don't know. She could sing and she was very good. ...'

I ask Mitch at what point he believed Amy might be able to have a professional career as a performer.

'... I want to do something with the talents I've been "blessed"
with ... Mostly, I have this dream to be very famous. .... I want
people to hear my voice and just ... forget their troubles for five
minutes...' – Amy Winehouse

Above: One of Amy's first live performances at the HMV store, Oxford Street, London, in January 2004.

Opposite: A young, healthy Amy at the Mercury Music Prize ceremony in September 2004.

Opposite: A fresh-faced Amy at the Mercury Music Prize Awards in September 2004.
Above: Amy's iconic style was set – as shown here at the BRIT Awards in February 2007.

Opposite: Amy and Blake in happier times at the 2007 MTV Awards in Los Angeles.

Amy's musical collaborations include this performance with superstar Mick Jagger at the Isle of Wight Festival, England, in June 2007 (**right**) and onstage with her *Back to Black* co-producer, Mark Ronson (**below**), at the BRIT Awards in 2008.

'She won a scholarship to go to Sylvia Young Drama School[4], which is one of the top drama schools in London, but she went as an actress and dancer. The singing was – I don't even know if they heard her sing and I think there was 800 applicants and there were two places and she won one of the places. ...

'My friend phoned me up, who is in show business, and said "Go out and buy *The Stage* [theatre paper]." ... So, I went to about 10 newsagents before I found *The Stage* and there it was – Amy ha[d] won a scholarship and there was a picture of her .... We thought "Wow, now things are starting to move forward a little bit", but even then we didn't think about her singing ... prior to that she had done a couple of pretty big acting jobs. She was at a theatre in a principal role, in a production as an actress, so that was more what we were really thinking, acting, maybe a little bit of dancing, tap dancing like Ginger Rogers, fabulous. ... She loved to dance, but at that stage again there really wasn't any sort of indication that she was a singer.'

Janis agrees with this when I interview her and Mitch together. '[Amy] was like the jolly kid, always a lovely, lovely child. She was like jolly and jumpy and happy and she was just enjoying it. And that was the most important thing. She enjoyed performing.'

'So, you never pushed her?' I ask Janis.

'No. And I always said, "What do you call a mother that's not a pushy Jewish mother" and she said, "*Mummy, that's you!*"'

Mitch says that if anyone was pushy it was his mother, Cynthia, who Amy loved, so much so that she has her Nan's name tattooed on her body. 'Amy was always, "Mum, I don't want to upset Nan,"' Janis adds.

'What about when she took her to the audition for *Annie*?' Mitch recalls. 'And there was a newspaper article the next day ... They sent her along, it wasn't Sylvia Young, it was Susi Earnshaw[5], the one before, and they told us and they told Amy we are only sending you [along] for experience because the key's not your key .... Somehow or other we forgot to tell my Mum about this. So, my Mum before Amy goes on the stage says "Now Amy, this is what you've got to do ..." ... but [Amy] said, "Nan, I'm only going for experience ...".

'Of course, the song's in the wrong key and she [Amy] comes off stage and my Mum wasn't nasty to her, but it was, "Amy, why couldn't you sing the song properly?", "Nan, I'm trying to explain to you, it's not my key. I'm only here for the experience."

'In the papers the next day, there was a review of the auditions and there was a whole section about pushy grandmothers and mothers. She [Cynthia] was [like], "You've got to do better." To my Mum if you put your mind to it you could do anything you want [sic]. Which obviously you can do – but you can't if it's in the wrong key.'

Cynthia's legacy is long-lasting and Amy frequently refers to her in interviews. We speak about Cynthia a few times in St Lucia and Amy tells me that she misses her still.

☆ ☆ ☆

When Amy applied to Sylvia Young, all the applicants were asked to write a short essay about themselves and their dreams. The 13-year-old Amy wrote, 'All my life I have been loud, to the point of being told to shut up. The only reason I have to be this loud is because you have to scream to be heard in my family. ... I've been told ... I have a lovely voice ... I want to do something with the talents I've been "blessed" with. ... Mostly, I have this dream to be very famous. ... I want people to hear my voice and just ... forget their troubles for five minutes. ...'

At Sylvia Young, where Amy stayed for three years until 2000, she became good friends with Tyler James, a singer–songwriter, who later would help give her career a welcome boost.

Sylvia Young immediately spotted the young girl's potential, commenting that Amy's talent could have put her in the same league as Judy Garland or Ella Fitzgerald, but all was not completely well for Amy at the school. She was incredibly clever, but she was bored when she wasn't performing and was often disruptive. She wouldn't wear her uniform properly, had a nose ring and chewed gum in lessons.

It was about this time that Mitch also noticed Amy had began to act up in earnest. ' ... Maybe she was 14, and she would stay out all night. I had to go and find her and I was convinced that she was dead ... I am morbid. That is the way that my mind works unfortunately.

'I would be driving through the streets of North London looking for her, knocking on people's doors ... Completely irrational, but that's the way you are where your children are concerned.'

I ask him if he thought Amy did it on purpose. 'It's possible. I don't think so. I don't think Amy has ever thought through the consequences of her actions. [Has] never taken responsibility for her actions. I don't think she was any different to how she is now.'

At school, however, the teachers had had enough of Amy's behaviour, it seemed. Janis recalls, 'I got called into school ... and the head teacher there said to me, "Well, Amy's not doing what she could do ... academically. She's a very, very bright girl, should be doing such and such ... And he's talking all the talk, but saying "Find her another school."'

It would have been a tough moment for any parent, I say, having not only their child but themselves as parents judged by this teacher.

Mitch continues, 'Sylvia Young now will say that didn't happen, but it did ... But basically she [Amy] was asked to leave. ...

'In the normal academic school, 100 percent of the day is taken up with studying, apart from the physical activities. At this stage school, it's probably two-thirds stage work, music and dancing and a third academia and Amy ... just messed around. She couldn't wait to get back into the performance so she was asked to leave. ... We sent her to another private school and she made their life there hell for them.'

I ask Janis and Mitch if they were angry with Amy.

No,' Mitch says. 'You could never be angry with her ... There are children who are nasty and they are malicious. She was never malicious. You know, she just laughs, even now ....'

Janis adds, 'And that's how she *is* with problems ....'

☆ ☆ ☆

After leaving the Mount, in Mill Hill, North London, with five GCSEs, Amy moved to the BRIT School for Performing Arts & Technology in Croydon, Surrey, in South England, where she lasted less than a year. While there, she started singing with the National Youth Jazz Orchestra and performed in jazz clubs. In her spare time, she was hanging out with Juliette Ashby, her old friend from Southgate. She was also, by her own account, smoking marijuana.

Amy's voice was drawing increasing amounts of attention. In 2001, her old friend Tyler James was signed to Brilliant, a division of Simon Fuller's talent agency, 19 Entertainment Ltd. Knowing that manager Nick Godwin and A&R man Nick Shymansky were looking for a jazz singer, Tyler gave them a tape of Amy's.

Godwin says, 'We put it on and there was this amazing voice, fantastic lyrics. They were eight- or nine-minute poems, really. Quite awkward guitar playing, but utterly breathtaking.'

Mitch recalls that's when he understood that she could really sing, when 19 were interested in signing her to their management company. 'She was under 18, I had to sign for her. So I went up to the offices and they explained what they were going to do for her and they explained they already had offers from five, six publishing companies, five or six recording companies who were interested in signing Amy and we signed with them ….

'What was going through my mind was that Amy by now had left the stage school and she was in a situation where she had to earn money to live and she was also at the time working for an Internet News Agency, a company called "WENN" [through Juliette Ashby's father]. She was writing articles as a journalist there ... getting about £150 a week or something in those days, not enough to live on, so I was having to give her extra money, which you do as a parent. You do as a parent right?

'She was okay. She had enough money to get by. ... There were fairly decent advances. Nothing to retire on, but enough to enable her not to work anymore – and enough so that I didn't have to give her any money anymore. She could look after herself from the advances and ... she had five or six offers from all different kinds of recording companies and they settled on Island Records[6], which is a part of Universal .... They are people who nurture their talent ... and they are not looking for an album every six months. They are looking for longevity in their artists and they saw that in Amy ... somebody who perhaps could have a long career ....

'There ... was no pressure on her to produce the album quickly. They said take your time, no problem, we will support you or help you and finally she produced her first album, which was *Frank* and it is my favourite album.

'She only produced two albums, but I prefer *Frank* to ... *Back To Black*, because *Back To Black* deals with certain subjects, which I am uncomfortable with. Whereas the first album ... was pretty innocent.'

what is it
about men

If you believe in luck, then Amy's luck was at its height when she met Nick Shymansky, 19 Entertainment Ltd's A&R man, and they began working together. From the beginning Shymansky realized that Amy's talent would be best nurtured if she worked with a producer who understood her voice, background, range and diverse influences – from TLC, Mos Def and Nas to Frank Sinatra and Sarah Vaughan – and who could help her develop her songs and lyrics. Amy's choice was a West London-based producer named Major, who had worked with trip-hop legend Tricky[1]. Shymansky brought them together.

Major and Amy worked hard together from the first time they met in September 2001, creating mesmerizing and attention-grabbing music – songs in which Amy would, with often disarming and heartbreaking honesty, document her life, her thoughts and her world for everyone to hear.

It was for this that Amy would become best known, particularly after the release of her album *Frank*, which she recorded after being signed by Darcus Beese, the influential A&R man at Island Records and Major's friend.

☆ ☆ ☆

Frank's production and road to release wasn't a smooth one, however. In 2002, manager Nick Godwin arranged for Amy to work with a pair of young songwriters, Stefan Skarbek and Matt Rowe. Composer Felix Howard also occasionally worked with them. At the time, Amy was also experimenting with music, listening to all types and genres, from music picked up on shopping trips to shops like Oxfam in Kentish Town.

Amy, Skarbek and Rowe ended up recording a lot of material for what they thought would be her debut album. Some of the music they produced during that time shows Amy's quirky sense of humour and observations of life. Word games between Amy and the boys formed the mainstay of the lyrics for the songs that they produced together.

As it became increasingly likely that Amy would sign with Island records, the pressure increased to have a unified, clear body of music that could form the basis of a successful debut album.

Eventually Amy signed a publishing deal with EMI Music Publishing Ltd, and with the advance from that agreement moved into a flat in Camden, North London, with her old friend Juliette Ashby, where Amy cooked, wrote and the girls both smoked dope. By December 2002, shortly after her 19th birthday, Amy's luck – or talent –

resulted in her being a fully contracted member of the Universal–Island Records stable.

In the end, only 'October Song', a track apparently inspired by the death of the pet canary that Amy had forgotten to feed when she went away for a weekend, and 'Amy, Amy, Amy' made it onto *Frank* from the sessions with Skarbek and Rowe.

Co-produced by the brilliant Miami-based Salaam Remi[2] and New Jersey-based Commissioner Gordon, most of the songs on *Frank* are inspired by the heartache and pain caused by the break-up of Amy's relationship with Chris Taylor.

'I constantly want to look after people', she said later, 'but I've only met a couple of men in my life who deserved or appreciated it. My first proper long-term boyfriend Chris (he's the fella that I wrote my first album about) was lovely, but he didn't really appreciate it.'

☆ ☆ ☆

'Did you like Chris?'

Mitch replies, 'Well, I didn't really know him. He was a decent enough guy from what I can remember of him, but she is writing [in *Frank*] about … her first love. It is pretty innocent. Things go a bit wrong. She tries to put it back on track. He tries to get it back on track … He should have been more of a man and she writes about this.

'She call[s] him a "lady boy", or "are you a lady boy"[3]? But … he understood the situation. He understood that there wasn't any malice in what Amy did and they still have got a pretty good relationship now.

'It's not everybody who can say they have had an album written about them, can they? ... But this boy can.'

'I really enjoy that album,' Mitch says. 'I think it's good ... the songs are great, although it didn't sell that many.'

Frank was actually a platinum-selling album. It was nominated for two BRIT Awards for British Female Solo Artist and British Urban Act, and 'Stronger Than Me' also won Amy the prestigious Ivor Novello Award for Best Contemporary Song.

'It got to No. 7 in the British Charts [*Frank* actually reached No. 13 in the UK Charts]. It wasn't released in America ... it's a well thought of, very critically acclaimed album. But it didn't sell because Amy wasn't as well known ... *Back To Black* sold 10 million copies, so that's a serious piece of work. I still prefer the first one.

'I feel more comfortable with [*Frank*] more because I know what went into it. ... That is why she is never going to be an Irving Berlin[4] ... [He] wrote 4,000 songs in his life. He wrote about one song every week and that is what he was able to do. ... Some of them ... we know ('White Christmas'), but some of them you wouldn't know and some ... are not very good at all. ... But Amy will never be able to do that ... Any song that she writes is like cutting an arm off. Every song is like pulling her heart out.'

'Why "cutting her arm off"?' I interject, 'I would say, like "giving birth".'

'Yeah, you are right,' he agrees. 'That is a much better way of putting it ... giving birth. Each song is a creation, which has come out of painful memories and painful experiences. It is not going to be a song about "how lovely the moon looks tonight" ... It's not going to be about that kind of stuff. So, that's why she really probably needs two to three years to write an album.'

☆ ☆ ☆

In the lead-up to *Frank*'s release, Amy performed live three times at the 4 Sticks Live nights at the Cobden, a private members club in West London, where many live bands have performed. Acclaimed musician Annie Lennox caught one of Amy's performances. She told *The Times*, 'I saw her at the Cobden Club when she was 18, and I was completely blown away. She was like a woman in her thirties, with a whole, seasoned delivery, not fazed by anything at all. I was in awe of her. I thought, wow, you have a special talent. God, you are 18, where did that come from?'

In October 2003, Island released 'Stronger Than Me' as a single. Despite being pushed by Island and receiving attention from critics who were intrigued by Amy's unique sound, the song only reached No. 71 in the UK charts. *Frank* was released later that month and Amy found herself heralded as the new girl in Britain's 'new jazz' movement, along with such musicians as Jamie Cullum and Norah Jones.

☆ ☆ ☆

The subject matter of most of the songs on *Frank*, Amy's ex-boyfriend, immediately brought her a lot of media attention, as did the originality of her music and the influence and mixture of different and, to some critics, contradictory music genres, including jazz.

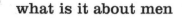

Favourably reviewed by most of the major British press (the *Guardian* compared her sound on *Frank* as sitting between Nina Simone and Erykah Badu, at once 'innocent and sleazy'; the *Daily Telegraph* commented 'she writes like Cole Porter, sings like Billie Holiday, plays snooker like a pro'), Amy continued to perform live, supporting Jamie Cullum and opening for Finley Quaye. In December 2003, she took to the stage in her first major solo showcase since the Cobden, at the famous Shepherd's Bush venue, Bush Hall, to an audience of over 300 people. Her reviews were mixed, however – her performance described by some as confused and nervous.

Without a doubt Amy was beginning to catch the attention of the media, sometimes for her talent, sometimes for her comments. In an interview with MusicOMH.com, she made it clear that she didn't like being lumped together with Jamie Cullum and Katie Melua, just because their records came out at the same time. While adding that she felt bad for Jamie who must feel frustrated, she said of Katie, 'SHE must think it's her f**king lucky day.'

Musically though, Amy was receiving critical attention from her peers and the public as well. Nominated for two BRIT Awards (British Female Solo Artist/British Urban Act), on 17 February 2004, she lost in both categories to Dido and Lemar respectively, but Amy was grabbing attention and to the media and her public she seemingly appeared more confident and more self-assured with every interview she gave.

Appearing on *The Jonathan Ross Show* in March 2004, a beautiful Amy – hair sleek and slim but curvaceous in a form-fitting short halter neck dress and high heels –

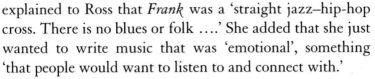

explained to Ross that *Frank* was a 'straight jazz–hip-hop cross. There is no blues or folk ....' She added that she just wanted to write music that was 'emotional', something 'that people would want to listen to and connect with.'

In that interview, Amy comes across as a normal, bright, lovely young woman, sure of her own opinions and views. Only the occasional movement of her hands betrays possible nervousness or just her youth. When Ross asks if her management company had tried to change her – her look, her way of speaking or behaviour – she jokes to the audience that someone tried to mould her into a big triangle shape and that she said 'No-oh!', to much laughter from everyone around her, Ross included. She then continues more seriously, 'No, I've got my own style and I wrote my own songs and, you know, if someone has so much of something already, there's very little you can add.'

Watching Amy give a mesmerising performance of 'I Heard Love Is Blind' from *Frank* at the end of that interview, playing an acoustic guitar, it's hard to equate that self-assured and alluring young woman with the one who I meet in St Lucia in 2009.

So, I have to ask myself, what happened to Amy? When did things begin to go wrong? What caused this train wreck to happen? Do the reasons lie in her past? And why could – or did – no one stop her? I think about my first meeting with Janis, when she very bluntly, almost cruelly, says 'I cannot help Amy unless she helps herself.' Does that have something to do with it?

☆ ☆ ☆

'Do you remember the first time you felt "Wow, something else is going on in her life?"'

'Well, you know,' Mitch replies. 'I have to say first of all, and it is well documented, that when she was interviewed about drugs, she was anti Class A drugs.

'Since the age of about 17,' he continues, 'she smoked weed or marijuana, or whatever you call it, but not to the extent that it would make her psychotic – to relax and whatever. I don't personally agree with it, that is something she has done.'

He adds that neither he nor Janis has tried it.

'… Were you aware [at the time] that she was trying light drugs, like marijuana?' I ask.

'No. I think that Janis kind of kept that from me. When the first album came out, there is a picture of her [Amy] … on the album and my friend said to me, "You know she is rolling a spliff" [joint], and I said, "What are you talking about?"… I didn't even know what a spliff was.

'I said [to Amy], "Are you smoking marijuana?" And she said, "Oh, Dad, don't be silly."

'I said, "I am not happy about that." She said, "I am over 18, Dad. I can do what I like."

'So, what can I do?' Mitch asks me. 'She is over 18. I can't lock her up.'

☆ ☆ ☆

During my time with the Winehouses I'm struck by the different approaches that Mitch and Janis take to their daughter's problems. Although Mitch states that he can't 'lock her up', he is always keeping an eye on Amy. Her

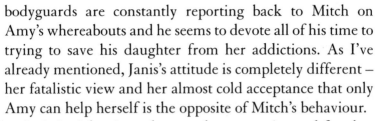

bodyguards are constantly reporting back to Mitch on Amy's whereabouts and he seems to devote all of his time to trying to save his daughter from her addictions. As I've already mentioned, Janis's attitude is completely different – her fatalistic view and her almost cold acceptance that only Amy can help herself is the opposite of Mitch's behaviour.

Janis is right. Amy does need to recognize and face her own problems in order to start recovering but perhaps both these attitudes, however well-intended, are too extreme. For Amy to overcome her addictions she needs to get proper treatment. As I've discovered through my extensive interviews with other celebrities who suffer with addictions, rehab only works when the whole family is involved and opens up. But from what I've seen of the Winehouse family, it is clear that they are not ready to do this.

Maybe they don't understand that this is what's needed? Or maybe they dread having to go down this route? Either way, anything less than full rehab treatment is only a quick fix for Amy.

☆ ☆ ☆

Mitch emphasizes the fact that at that time Amy declared publicly in several interviews that she was opposed to Class A drugs. 'She said that "Anybody who takes Class A drugs is a 'mug'." Now a "mug" in English terminology is someone who is stupid – and, of course, she didn't take Class A drugs.'

'Were you convinced?' I *have* to ask him.

'It wasn't a question of being convinced,' he replies. 'That was the truth. ...'

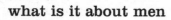

'At that point you didn't think something was wrong?'
I persist.

'There wasn't anything wrong, apart from her smoking marijuana. It wasn't only me saying that. People who know her. Her friends. They confirmed that she was a complete opponent of Class A drugs. She would not take Class A drugs. She regarded anyone who took [them] as a fool. She didn't want to be in their company. Then, unfortunately she did meet somebody who did take Class A drugs.

'And the rest, as they say, is history.'

you know i'm no good

By the end of 2004, Amy should have been riding on a high. She'd seen her debut album go platinum and received critical success with nominations for the BRITs and the Ivor Novello awards, the latter of which she'd won. She'd performed at Glastonbury Festival in June on the Jazz World Stage and at V in August. September had seen her sing at the prestigious Mercury Music Prize awards in London for which she had herself received a nomination, along with other rising stars such as Franz Ferdinand, The Streets, Belle and Sebastian and Snow Patrol. It was good company to be amongst, even though she lost to Franz Ferdinand.

Amy had also gone on two UK tours and she was now showing the world that she was an artist – and a woman – to be reckoned with. But now Island Records was asking: what next?

Amy had begun to think about her second album, but what could she write about? What would inspire her? She wrote about the world as she experienced it after all? Her life, her friends, her loves, her disappointments. What would be next?

She apparently found her answer at her local pub in Camden, the Hawley Arms, where she often played pool and listened to a lot of '50s and '60s music on the jukebox. There, in early 2005, she met a man who, quite literally, would change her life, Blake Fielder-Civil.

Blake was Amy's ideal type – 'at least five nine, with dark hair, dark eyes and loads of tattoos.'

Their relationship was turbulent from the offset and continued to be so for the intense six months that it lasted until Blake went back to his girlfriend. Amy later commented that she shouldn't have got involved with him in the first place as Blake was involved with someone else 'too close to home.'

☆ ☆ ☆

Mitch and Janis both talk to me about Amy's relationship with Blake when they first met.

'Well, she wasn't dating him. They didn't date,' Janis denies.

'No,' Mitch comments. 'He was seeing somebody else. What happened was that he [Blake] started to see Amy for the first time on a casual basis just after *Frank* came out. But, of course, after six months, the interest [in the album] started waning a little bit, so it seemed that Blake's interest in Amy started to wane a bit … He was

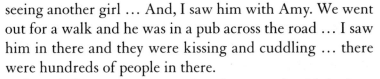
seeing another girl … And, I saw him with Amy. We went out for a walk and he was in a pub across the road … I saw him in there and they were kissing and cuddling … there were hundreds of people in there.

'I said, "Amy, I'm not saying that you shouldn't show affection, but he's somebody else's boyfriend anyway and you really don't want to be doing that in a room …." I was quite sensitive about things like that. And she said, "Dad, you're right." So, we left and you know, that was really the first time that I saw him and he didn't turn up again until *Back To Black* was No. 1."'

'She wrote a lot of those songs [about] him,' Janis comments.

'The second album?' I ask.

'Yes, that's right,' she confirms.

'That's why,' Mitch interjects, 'I don't like to listen to it ….'

☆ ☆ ☆

Under pressure from her record company to get into a studio and record her second album, and heartbroken over Blake, Amy began to spiral out of control. Summing up that time, she said, 'My ex went back to his girlfriend and I went back to drinking and dark times.'

Island Records suggested that she needed to cut down on her drinking and Amy's friends and family began to worry about her boozing and also the amount of weight she was losing.

☆ ☆ ☆

I ask Janis about that time during one of our discussions. I ask her when she first realized that her daughter was in trouble.

'... She was losing weight,' Janis murmurs. '... She really was. And ... what Amy always does is deny ... I would say, "Amy, why are you losing weight?" ... I'd been informed that Amy was bringing up her food.'

'She was bulimic?' I ask.

'Bulimic, yes ... I can remember Amy saying to me that she'[d] got a great diet ... "Well, you get the food and you chew it and get the taste of it; then you swallow the taste and spit it [the food] out." And she even told Mitch that. "Look, Dad, there's a really good diet..."'

I'm very surprised to hear this story from Janis. I would imagine that hearing these kind of comments from your daughter would be a mother's worst nightmare. I find it strange that Janis wasn't more alarmed by Amy's issues with her weight and her relationship with food.

Janis continues, '... I believe the time we really knew she was throwing up was when she performed at a friend's wedding and she was eating very well, but she was taking herself to the toilet and bringing it up. ... It was heard ... It all seemed to get out of control.'

Certainly, some British papers also picked up on Amy's changed appearance, commenting on the amount of time Amy was spending in the gym – and also on her alleged image issues since the release of *Frank*.

When I ask Mitch about Amy's weight loss, he says, 'She had that [bulimia] for some time, but certainly I would say from the time of the first album [*Frank*] ... 2004 and 2005. She lost a lot of weight, which thankfully she has put back on. She is like her Mum. Her Mum is slim and I am not ....'

Mitch adds that he told Amy many times that she needed to do something about the bulimia, 'And she did. ... She sought counselling ... My understanding of [that] is they are teaching people how to eat again. How to keep the food down. We all know that it is not about food at all. It is generally about self-image. It is about how people are feeling about themselves.'

'... She clearly found difficulties in dealing with her success. There is no question about it and I think the bulimia was merely the first stage of what would become a serious problem.'

I comment that bulimia and anorexia often stop the sufferer from menstruating. In many cases the sufferers don't want to be treated as women; they want to be treated like little kids. Did he see Amy experiencing any of that?

'I am not a doctor or a psychiatrist,' he says. 'But I would say that would be fairly accurate. She has found it difficult doing what she has done for so many reasons and maybe deep inside her mind, she would prefer it to be as it was. A lot less complicated when she was 14 years old ...'

☆ ☆ ☆

In the end, Amy went to see an addiction counsellor. She told the *Sun* in 2006 that she'd asked Mitch if she 'needed' to go to rehab and he told her 'No', but to give it a try. Amy followed her Dad's advice, but only stayed long enough to explain to the counsellor that she drank because she'd been in love and 'fucked up the relationship' before walking out.

She believed if she couldn't help herself, she couldn't be helped at all.

Drawing on her experiences, Amy wrote one of the songs with which she would become most associated, and also the one that would catapult her from being a 'new jazz' artist to a mainstream, internationally known and respected musician. It was 'Rehab'. This track eventually appeared on *Back To Black*.

With several songs already written, most drawing on her relationship with Blake, it seemed likely to Island and Raye Cosbert at the Camden-based Metropolis Music, who now managed Amy, that she might finally be ready to get into a studio and start recording again. Salaam Remi, who had worked on *Frank*, was on board and Island's Darcus Beese decided to mix things up a bit and get a new co-producer involved. He introduced Amy to the much talked-about and eclectic DJ and producer Mark Ronson.

Although Amy had initial reservations about working with Ronson, in fact, the couple had a lot in common – both were born in London (although Ronson subsequently moved to the States, where he was brought up), both are Jewish, and both have a great affinity to, and respect for, black music. The latter, in particular, shows through strongly on *Back To Black*.

According to Ronson, Amy played him a whole load of 'really cool' music that she loved from the '50s and '60s, including the Shangri-Las, Tony Bennett and the Cadillacs. Inspired, Ronson sent her away and started messing around with a tambourine and a piano, creating overnight what would become the main sketch for 'Back To Black', the title track of the album. Ronson later commented that it was hard to tell if Amy liked it when he first played it to her as she doesn't, in general, really get excited – but then she murmured, 'It's wicked!'

Once the first track was set, Ronson and Amy worked hard to lay the basis for the rest of the tracks. As before, Amy worked with two producers and moved between New York, where Ronson was based, and Miami, to work with Remi, creating the vintage sound that works so successfully on the album, particularly on tracks like 'Love Is A Losing Game'. The final mood of the album both complements Amy's sultry voice and heartfelt lyrics and also is nostalgic in the sense that this was the kind of music she was listening to when she first hung out with Blake in the Hawley Arms.

Commenting on the difference in sound and tone between *Frank* and *Back To Black*, Amy said, 'I wrote my first album when I was listening to a lot of jazz, a lot of hip-hop …. [On] my second album, I was listening to a substantially smaller amount of music – soul, doo-wop, girl groups – and it shows.'

☆ ☆ ☆

'I don't like to listen to it …,' Mitch says of the album. 'The song "Back To Black" … it's about going back into depression and when [Blake's] not there, she's depressed and when he's there, she's not …

'And it's well documented how I view the relationship [with Blake] being totally … destructive. It's not a good relationship … of course, I don't want my daughter to be depressed either ….

'... As I've told you she's never going to be writing songs about how beautiful the moon is ... each song that she writes is giving birth. Some of them are positive; some are negative. It's a great album but you know I personally view it as a period of depression for her, which she is coming out of slowly.

'Let's hope the next album is going to be a little bit more cheerful – I doubt it ....'

☆ ☆ ☆

In its first week of sales, *Back To Black* sold more than 40,000 copies in the UK, after which its sales increased, pushing it up the album chart until it reached No. 1. Amy's career was, it seemed, made.

The reviews were fantastic. Amy was compared to Etta James and Edith Piaf, and she was praised for leaving behind the laid-back lounge influences of her former album and strutting into 'gloriously ballsy, bell-ringing, bottle-swigging, doo-wop territory.'

Amy's star was certainly ascending and, on the domestic front, she seemed happy, too, having met a new man, Alex Claire. He was seemingly the antithesis to Blake: blond to Amy's preferred type of 'dark hair, dark eyes.' Alex moved in with Amy within a month of meeting her and she claimed publicly, as she would do with Blake and others in her life later, that Alex was her 'best mate.'

Ever frank, she also talked about her weight loss, blaming it on her healthier lifestyle, after she stopped smoking '£200 worth of weed a week, that's two ounces' and began going to the gym. However, within days the press was going mad after Amy made a rather startling appearance on *The Charlotte Church Show*[1]; she was seemingly disorientated and forgot the words to Michael Jackson's 'Beat It'. The British tabloids reported that she was extremely drunk and had been asked by her label to cut down on her alcohol consumption. Many stories and rumours began to surface about her weight loss and eating disorders.

In November 2006, Amy set out on another UK tour, this time to promote the album. Most of the early reviews of her gigs focus on her changed appearance and her weight loss, one commenting that she had changed from a curvy teen to an 'emaciated fitness addict.'

Amy's bad girl image was also gaining credence at great speed, fuelled by a fracas with a member of her audience at one of her gigs and a much recounted appearance on *Never Mind the Buzzcocks,* when host Simon Amstell awkwardly joked about Amy coming onto the show full of 'crack' and concluded that the show wasn't a pop quiz anymore but rather an 'intervention.'

Amy was still proclaiming that she was 'weed-free' and much healthier, a result of Alex's calming effect on her lifestyle. She admitted freely that she still loved to drink, but her relationship with Alex had made her realize that she was a bad and violent drunk.

☆ ☆ ☆

2007 began with a bang. Amy played to rave reviews and an A-list music audience, including Jay-Z and Mos Def, at Joe's Pub in New York. She embarked on a UK tour and was nominated in February 2007 for a BRIT Award for British Female Solo Artist, which she won, modestly thanking her parents in her speech.

Back To Black still topped the UK album charts and had sold more than half a million copies and Island had scheduled a US release for it in March of that year. But all was not well. Amy's behaviour was becoming increasingly erratic and she was starting to miss performances.

At this point, Mitch tells me that he started to realize that something was really up with his daughter. 'The thing that she loves to do more than anything else is to perform live. ... Clearly at that stage things were going wrong.'

He describes one particular incident, '... She was actually walking onto the plane and she turned around and walked off ... that cost her about £80,000. It was a considerable amount of money,' adding, '... And there was a performance [later] in Paris that cost her maybe a £100,000 ... It [was] extremely damaging.'

He continues, 'I went to meet her after she came off the plane and I was with her manager ... I sat down with her and I explained ... that it was going to cost her and she didn't care. For whatever the reason was she just didn't want to do that performance. ... It was extremely worrying and at that stage we didn't know how successful the album was going to be. We didn't know it was going to be the best-selling album of 2007 so we really felt that her cancelling a gig and that costing her £100,000, that could make or break her. So ... I [was] thinking to myself, "Well, my daughter is going to be in a position where she isn't going to have any money."

'"She is going to be this superstar with absolutely no money." And that concerned me as well.

'Although we don't care about money per se … you wouldn't want to be without it.'

☆ ☆ ☆

I know that there are many people who consider Mitch to be capitalizing on his daughter's fame and enjoying a luxurious lifestyle at her expense. While I do believe that Mitch really cares about Amy and would do anything to help her, I think that the money is a real issue. Mitch brings up Amy's finances in our interviews and it does seem to be an important topic for him.

When I first met Mitch and we began this project together, he was not in full control of Amy's money. He did, in fact, consult us at the time about whether he should take charge of Amy's finances and it seems that while Amy was in hospital in November 2008, the step was taken to put Mitch and Janis in control. I don't doubt that he had good intentions and, at that point, I thought it was a good idea, as it would help to stop Amy spending her money on drugs – something that Mitch has said to me just wasn't possible while Amy was accountable for her own money.

With hindsight, it raises a lot of questions for me. Mitch is adamant that Amy is now free of drugs and has overcome her addiction but if this is the case why does Mitch still feel the need to control his daughter in this way? If Amy is healthy and clean, then it doesn't make sense for her parents to still be in charge of her own money.

☆ ☆ ☆

I ask Mitch if he and Amy are close.

'VERY close,' he answers.

So, I say, when you started to notice something was wrong, what did you put her behaviour down to.

'I am not an expert in drug addiction,' he replies, '… in how people react when they have taken drugs, but it seemed that she wasn't her normal self … It was more of a father's intuition that things weren't right. It wasn't only her behaviour; it was the things that were happening in her life. Performances were starting to be not as good as they were. Some were being missed.'

'Did you confront her?' I persist. 'Did you say, "Honey, what's going on?"'

'No. No. I didn't. No, I didn't confront her. … With hindsight, perhaps I should have done.'

there is no greater love

Amy was already well on the way to becoming known as much for her appearance (beehive, heavily kohl-ringed eyes and tattooed body – her tattoos include 'Blake's', positioned just above her heart, from their earlier six-month relationship, an anchor emblazoned with the words 'Hello Sailor' and another proclaiming her 'Daddy's Girl'), attitude and alleged alcohol- and drug-fuelled benders, as for her talent as a musician.

Behind the scenes, Amy's love life was also unravelling. Her nine-month relationship with Alex came to an end in early 2007, but within weeks, about the time that *Back To Black* was released in North America and Amy embarked on a tour of the States and Canada, she and Blake were seeing each other again.

Janis tells me that she spoke to Amy about Alex and Blake at that time and that Amy was definitely upset about the break-up. But, she adds: '[Amy] was just excited at seeing [Blake]. It was Easter and she went over to America with Blake to New York and she'd fought with … Alex the day before she went … I finally got hold of her and I said, "Amy, how are you?" and she said, "I'm so upset, Mum. I am so hurt. I have broken up with Alex and it has really distressed me."

'I said, "Oh, Amy. Is that why you went with Blake to New York?" And there was no answer.'

'She didn't know that you knew. How did you find out?' I query.

'Oh, I knew, because those are things that I know. I knew she was with Blake.'

'[Amy] knew that you disapproved?'

'Yes.'

☆ ☆ ☆

I have to admit that before I committed to doing the documentary, certainly well before I had begun to research Amy's life and family, I hadn't heard of Blake Fielder-Civil at all. Over the next months, though, I was to learn more than I could possibly have envisaged about Blake and Amy's addictive but seemingly destructive relationship – and also about how the Winehouses and Amy herself felt about it.

After hearing Mitch and Janis's initial impressions of Blake, which were certainly not favourable, and looking back through the transcripts of our discussions, I have to question how much Mitch and Janis, as parents, are complicit in what happened to Amy after she got back together with Blake.

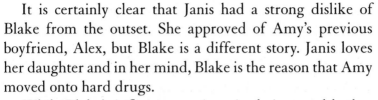

It is certainly clear that Janis had a strong dislike of Blake from the outset. She approved of Amy's previous boyfriend, Alex, but Blake is a different story. Janis loves her daughter and in her mind, Blake is the reason that Amy moved onto hard drugs.

While Blake's influence on Amy is obvious and he has even admitted that he did introduce Amy to hard drugs, I think it is more complicated than that – their relationship is a co-dependency of two addicted people. But for Janis, it is quite simple: Blake is to blame for Amy's addiction – and she hates him for it.

And, one has to question why did neither Mitch nor Janis step in at an earlier stage when they saw the warning signs after meeting Blake? Why didn't they individually or together call Amy to account about her behaviour? Why did they seemingly sit by and let their daughter flounder on alone, getting ever more deeply embroiled in her addictions?

☆ ☆ ☆

When I broach the subject of Blake with Mitch, he says: 'I heard about him about the middle of 2006.' He has already commented on seeing Blake and Amy together in a London pub, but now he adds, 'Amy and Blake were having a kind of on/off relationship and Blake was seeing another girl, who he obviously preferred to Amy and he didn't feel he could leave this other girl … When Amy started to become successful and when she started to do well, he joined Amy. He started going [out] with Amy in 2007 … and I met him. She was doing a show in Bayswater [West London] ….'

'When was that?' I ask.

'Around about March 2007. ... My first impression was that he was a nice guy. Very friendly. He shook my hand. He was very polite and he seemed ... very pleasant ....'

'What did he say?' I am intrigued. '... Did he say – "I love your daughter?"'

'No!' Mitch exclaims. 'Nothing like that. He didn't give a big speech or anything. He said, "I am Blake" and "It's nice to meet you ... I am looking forward to the show tonight."'

'Did you know who he was?' I question.

'I knew *of* him .... I knew at that point, [Amy] was seeing him. And she kind of sort of made moves to get us together .... *At that point* I had no good reason not to get together with him. None whatsoever. I am very welcoming as far as Amy's boyfriends are concerned.'

'So, when was the next time ...?'

'The next time ... was when we went to New York to do the *Letterman Show*. David Letterman. We flew together and I was with him for five to six days. ... He went out to join her. She was already there doing a mini tour ... and she wanted him to be there.'

'So, she paid for the ticket?' I say quizzically.

'Of course,' Mitch replies.

I find his quiet acceptance that this is OK interesting and tell him so, adding: 'Well, I'm very successful and I don't pay for my boyfriend.'

'Well, you might do if he didn't have any visible means of income ...,' Mitch responds sarcastically.

'I am not so sure,' I argue.

'Well, she did.'

I have to pursue this further. 'It didn't bother you at that point?'

'*At that point*,' he says, 'it wasn't a problem. In fact maybe she didn't even pay [at all] because I think the record company sends us out, or something like that. I can't even remember.'

I am surprised that this situation doesn't concern Mitch more. A new relationship – one moreover that he's suspicious about – and he doesn't seem concerned that his daughter or her record label might be footing the bill for this new man's expenses. He even seems to think it's reasonable.

So, I repeat the question again: 'It didn't bother you *at that point*?'

'No,' he repeats. 'It didn't bother me at that point. Not at all.'

OK.

'You flew together. It's a long flight. It takes seven hours to get to New York,' I state.

'We weren't sitting together …,' Mitch says. 'I went First Executive, or something like that, and they stuck him back in [economy class] …. I said to him I really need to have a sleep, so I had a sleep … I woke up and I went back and I spoke to him for about half an hour to an hour and he seemed like a decent guy.'

'Maybe you should have spent seven hours with him?' I say, thinking maybe then he wouldn't have seemed such a 'decent guy'.

'Maybe I should have. But I didn't,' he says.

☆ ☆ ☆

It strikes me that Mitch is in denial about Amy – maybe this is because he loves her and he really wants to grab onto any glimmer of hope that Amy is okay – but, in my mind, he is in constant denial.

Amy is doing what she is doing and there are many reasons for her behaviour, but Mitch doesn't push his daughter to find out what possesses her to act as she often does – or, indeed, to try to find out what demons drive her. Mitch's refusal to accept the reality of the situation forms part of that addiction.

☆ ☆ ☆

News of Amy's relationship with Blake filtered back to England, and even though they had broken up, Alex didn't take the news at all well. He made his feelings known to anyone who would listen, as seen, in particular, when he sold alleged intimate details of his sex life with Amy to the press, an action that helped to strengthen Amy's 'bad girl', 'rock chick' image.

Amy seemed happy with Blake, however, and Blake joined her on a trip to Canada, where she was performing, about a month after the New York trip. It was then that Mitch first began to worry about Blake's influence on his daughter.

He says, '... [We] went to Canada and he was already there with Amy. ... We are talking about April 2007. Amy did maybe three or four shows ... but they did not move out of the room. They were in the room the whole time. And when she went to do the shows ... he was in the room, just all the time.'

'Did *that* bother you?' I ask.

Mitch concurs this time. 'That *did* concern me. Because at the time, being naive, I am thinking, "What is he doing in the room for all the time? Sleeping? He can't be sleeping all day." He was in the room 23 hours.'

'What did you do?' I say to him.

'Again we went about our business and I said to Amy, "Where's Blake? I haven't seen him. ..."'

'... When did you actually think, "Oh my God! My daughter is dating a drug addict? A hard drug addict?"' I say.

'... He was in the room and he never emerged. I don't know what he was doing in the room. I can only surmise what he was doing, but he never came out of the room. But Amy's situation, she never seemed to me at that point to be out of control. I saw two of her performances, which were absolutely superb, so she was able to perform and put on a good show. ... The problems started much later.'

'So when you reflect back that was probably the time?' I persist.

'Yeah, I would say so. With the benefit of hindsight I look back – yeah maybe, that's right.'

☆ ☆ ☆

In April 2007, Amy and Blake became engaged. The British tabloid the *Sun* was one of several newspapers to break the story, commenting that 'Caner Of the Year contender Amy' had decided that Blake was 'the one' and had recently been seen flashing her Tiffany ring

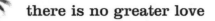

around to friends. Amy publicly referred to Blake as her 'boy' and also her 'best friend' – much in the same way that she'd referred to Alex Claire when they were together just a few months earlier.

I ask Janis if she was surprised by her daughter's engagement. Janis comments that when Amy introduced her to Blake, she 'took one look and said – "*He* is not somebody that she [Amy] should be with. *He* has nothing to offer!" … I was polite and when I heard the story that he'd asked her to marry him, well, I thought … she won't. She won't, because … I had been at her home and she said, "Mum, I don't think I am the marrying sort. I don't think it's for me … I'm not the sort to think of somebody else so I don't think I could work marriage."'

While on tour in the States though, Amy and Blake did get married in Miami; neither Mitch nor Janis were present.

'Did they elope?' I ask Janis.

'They didn't so much elope,' she says. '… I think it's just a weird story. They got married at … Miami-Dade County [Marriage License Bureau in Florida on 18 May] … And when I spoke to her I … heard that she had spoken to Mitch before that and he had said, "Don't get married Amy. Promise me you won't get married. Mum will be so upset."'

'Did she promise you?' I ask Mitch, intrigued by his answer.

Mitch responds: 'I knew she was going to get married [but] I didn't say "Don't get married." I said, "Don't get married without your Mother being there" because, Janis won't mind me telling you, when Janis and

I got married her mother wasn't there. And it was devastating. ...'

I turn to Janis. 'Were you devastated when your mother wasn't [at your wedding to Mitch]?'

Janis grimaces, 'No! I was quite happy actually ...'

Mitch interjects, '... Because Janis didn't get on with her Mum. I think I was more devastated for Janis ... being so close to my Mum ...'.

☆ ☆ ☆

'When did you know about the wedding?' I ask Mitch.

'... About half an hour after it happened,' he says. 'It wasn't a shock as I knew they were going to get married but I specifically asked Amy ... to make sure her Mum was there. ... But they chose to get married quickly and I was very upset. I *told* Amy I was upset.'

I comment that it was very generous of Mitch to worry so much about how Janis would feel when he's not married to her anymore. Most men wouldn't, they would just move forward.

'It is not a question of generosity ...' Mitch replies to me, 'As I explained, Janis and I, we ... remain very close. And I remember the anguish that Janis had when we got married and her Mum wasn't there and I didn't want her to go through that again. It was horrible for her. ...

'[Amy] phoned me about an hour and half after it happened. ... she was very excited. Of course I wasn't ..... I knew that I really wanted her Mum to be there. And *I* wanted to be there. I wanted our family to be there ...

But [Amy] didn't want the same things; she felt it was sufficient for them to be on their own.'

I ask Mitch what he said to her after she announced that she and Blake were married.

'I told her that her Mum was very upset and she said, "We will have a big party when we come home, Dad."

'We kind of got into that mind set that we would have a party when they got home [but] that is when the problems really started. From that date.'

☆ ☆ ☆

Blake and Amy spent a few days in Florida after their marriage. Mitch caught up with them both again after they returned to London. He tells me that he thinks this is the point at which things quickly began to deteriorate for Amy and his own relationship with his daughter began to change.

Before Amy's marriage to Blake Mitch was seeing his daughter three to four times a week but this now fell to about once a week. This was obviously difficult for Mitch to deal with.

Mitch said that he had to see Amy as there were certain things he had to discuss with her '… her business affairs. My signatures are on [her] account. I run the business on a day-to-day basis …. There are accountants and I have to discuss things with her [but] I couldn't get to see her. She was asleep … She was wrapped up with her husband – which is fair enough.

'I understand that when a young lady gets married she hasn't got as much time for her Dad as she used to have.

It is understandable. I [didn't] expect to see her three or four times a week.'

☆ ☆ ☆

On 9 August 2007, several newspapers ran the story that Amy had been rushed to a London hospital, where she had had her stomach pumped after a massive drugs overdose, something that Amy subsequently denied, but Blake Fielder-Civil confirmed in 2009, after his divorce from Amy.

Amy had, according to newspapers at that time, allegedly taken ecstasy, cocaine and ketamine (horse tranquillizers) during a London pub crawl, and washed it all down, at various points in the evening, with vodka and Jack Daniels.

When she started foaming at the mouth and fitting, Blake and a female friend (who Blake later confirmed was Juliette Ashby) took her to A&E.

Janis comments: 'If he'[d] have been in his normal state he wouldn't [have] … He *actually* had the presence of mind to turn her over on her side to stop her swallowing her tongue and on that occasion he saved her life … You can argue that his actions had brought Amy to this position, but on the one occasion he actually saved her life.

'Ironic isn't it?'

☆ ☆ ☆

Amy announced that her up-and-coming US tour would be delayed.

Mitch spoke to Blake's parents, Giles and Georgette, as they tried to work out how to help their children.

In the meantime, Amy was painfully thin as she hadn't been eating properly, was drinking too much and had an obvious problem with drugs, even if she didn't admit it herself. Mitch says, 'We weren't saying this is Blake's fault. They weren't saying this is Amy's fault. We weren't doing any of that. We were just trying to calm the troubled waters.'

They agreed that Amy would take 'me time' at a hotel near Fleet in Hampshire, South England.

'Amy ... was going to spend four or five days there with her best friends,' Mitch explains, 'which I thought ... would be great for her. I was going to stay there but I wasn't going to interfere, just to make sure everything was okay. We all really needed a rest because we had a very traumatic week one way or another. Amy was there the first day on her own, but then Blake turned up. ... Her friends disappeared because they had no time for Blake. They understood what his mission in life was. They decided they didn't want to be a party to it, and Blake was there and the whole time they didn't even come out of the room.

'So', I comment, 'you didn't even see your daughter?'

'It was difficult,' he says. 'They were in the room the whole time and [then] Blake's parents turned up .... We had a very nice meal with them the first evening. No problems at all.'

'With Amy and Blake [as well]?' I query.

'With Amy,' Mitch corrects. 'Blake was still in his room. Blake was still in bed. My impression, at that point, was that Blake's parents didn't understand the extent of his problems.'

I ask more about Blake's parents. What do they do?

'His stepfather is a deputy headmaster of a school and his mother is a hairdresser.'

'Are they nice people?' I say.

Mitch is strangely reticent. 'It's not for me to say – but *at the time* they seemed very nice people.'

I ask him if, in retrospect, he thinks the Fielder-Civils didn't like him.

'No,' he disagrees. 'At the time I think they seemed perfectly reasonable people who were working to resolve the problems of two newly married people ...

You were all trying to arbitrate, I suggest.

'... All trying to help and give them both support and my stance was that they both had to go into rehab. Before Blake got there, it was decided that Amy was going to go into rehab. ... Blake ... turned up and [now] Blake ha[d] to go into rehab as well. And, of course, all the doctors that we had down there and the clinical psychologists they all said the same thing. "You can't go into rehab together. It's foolish."'

He continues, '... Blake, at the time, didn't want to go into rehab. Amy had to go in, not only because of the drug situation, which at that time I don't think was the most important factor ... it was the eating disorder that was worse than anything. She was very poorly and malnourished. ... I think ... her peak weight [was] of about eight stone, she went down to about six-and-a-half stone. ... it was a considerable loss. ...

'In the morning I went into their room and I saw some drug paraphernalia and I reported this to Blake's stepfather and he just wouldn't accept it.

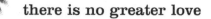

He said I was lying. ... I said [to him], "Are you telling me that Blake is not taking drugs?"

'So, there was an altercation and basically from that moment we have not been able to work with his parents. I am not saying anything about them. I am sure in their own way they are very nice people. Unfortunately we have had a terrible relationship with them. ... In fact it has got to a point where I ... had to instruct solicitors to basically tell them not to contact me because it did get very heated. They blame Amy for *everything*.'

I ask Mitch if he thinks Blake's parents were just in denial then.

He agrees, 'They are in denial. He is a fit young man and he is a healthy young man even though he takes drugs .... With Amy, if Amy takes drugs, because she is so little it hits her hard. You look at him and you look at her and it is like she is taking drugs and he doesn't.

'In their minds they are saying to themselves ... [that] he doesn't need to go [to rehab] and he was very concerned about Amy, in fairness to him. He was worried about her weight more than anything else. ... He was very supportive and helped her with her weight to the extent of when they were at rehab she put on 10 pounds in about five days. ... He was encouraging her, but in terms of the drug taking it was a complete waste of time.'

In August 2007, Blake and Amy both entered the exclusive rehab centre, The Causeway Retreat, situated on Osea island in Essex, England, about 40 miles from London.

Mitch is critical of the decision to allow his daughter and Blake, both deeply messed up at that point, to attend

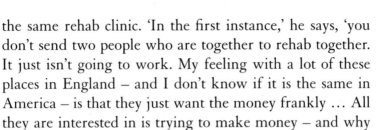

the same rehab clinic. 'In the first instance,' he says, 'you
don't send two people who are together to rehab together.
It just isn't going to work. My feeling with a lot of these
places in England – and I don't know if it is the same in
America – is that they just want the money frankly ... All
they are interested in is trying to make money – and why
shouldn't they? That is what makes the world go around.

'The first period of rehab was a waste of time, apart
from Amy's weight gain. They came back for a few days
and then they decided to go back again ... with varying
degrees of success. ...

'It was a horrible experience ... [The Causeway] is [on]
a small island off the coast of Essex and it is about
only half a mile off the mainland ... when the tide is
out there is a causeway that you can walk across, but
when the tide is in that is it, you are stuck there. The tide
at that time of the year came in about 12 o'clock at night
so, every night, the guy at the facility was phoning me
and he was saying to me that they want to come back.
They have sent for a car. So I said "Delay the car ..."
and then ... at about 12.30 say, "You can't go, that's it.
The tide is in and we can't get a vehicle across." ...
This ... happen[ed] for like seven days until eventually
that was it: they got off the island and that was the end
of the rehab.

'Basically it was a complete and utter waste of time.
What happened after that and what upset me most of all
was ... bearing in mind Amy and Blake had been in rehab
for drink and drug abuse, we had a meeting set up in
Chelsea ... [and Blake's] parents were coming down. We
had a car meet them at Kings Cross Station. That car was

then going to pick Amy and Blake up and come on to our meeting place …

He continues, 'We were in this meeting and we are waiting and there were eight people in there: the record company, solicitors, accountants, Amy's manager, Raye, [were] all waiting and … then we get a phone call. "We have decided not to come" – Blake's parents, they decided not to come … too much pressure. "We have decided to go out for a drink with [Amy and Blake].

'… This is about alcohol problems and now they are going out for a drink with them.

'We were all astonished and the next thing [the] paparazzi were all over them. There were photos of them coming out of pubs with their arms around each other and at that point we realized we couldn't work with *these people* [Blake's parents].

'Whatever their agenda is – and I am sure they care about their son and deep down I am sure they are fairly decent people – they won't acknowledge Blake's problems and they blame Amy for everything. Frankly, they hate Amy. They really *hate* Amy.'

This is a strong statement from Mitch and I do find myself wondering if it's true for him to say that Blake's parents really hate Amy. I did not meet Blake or his parents during the course of my interviews with the Winehouse family but it seems to me from everything I've heard that Blake does actually love Amy. In fact, from my interviews with both Janis and Mitch, it also sounds as if Blake has tried to reach out to them on some occasions.

I think that this says more perhaps about the issue of according blame between the two families. Of course,

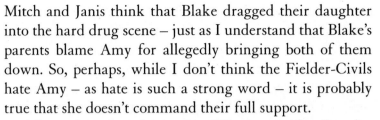

Mitch and Janis think that Blake dragged their daughter into the hard drug scene – just as I understand that Blake's parents blame Amy for allegedly bringing both of them down. So, perhaps, while I don't think the Fielder-Civils hate Amy – as hate is such a strong word – it is probably true that she doesn't command their full support.

After observing how the Winehouse family also interacts with one another, I think that perhaps this lack of support is a common factor in Amy's life and could be part of the reason for many of her insecurities and problems.

When you look at it on paper, Amy should have some really good female role models within her family: Janis, a single mother who raised two children and who is a very brave woman, coping with MS – and also, her step-mother Jane, who is a strong, working woman, seemingly understanding of Amy's problems and of the time Mitch has to spend dealing with them.

However, in reality, it seems to be all about the world of Mitch and Amy. The other family members are around and they care about Amy, of course, but it is only the dynamic between father and daughter that seems to be important. This hasn't left much room for either of these women to have played – or to play – an influential role in Amy's life.

☆ ☆ ☆

Amy and Blake checked themselves into the exclusive Central London hotel, the Sanderson, after leaving their rehab at The Causeway. Mitch had dinner with the couple later that night at the hotel.

Then, in the early hours of the morning of 23 August 2007, guests reported sounds of an altercation in the couple's hotel room and the police were called. Amy reportedly ran out of the hotel at about 3.30 a.m., chased by Blake, who appeared to have scratch marks on his neck. The couple ended up running down Regent Street, where Amy flagged down a passing car and drove off.

Blake eventually returned to the hotel, where he made several phone calls. He left the hotel again, this time returning with Amy at about 4.30 a.m. No charges were made but the couple are alleged to have had a £3,000 cleaning bill from the hotel.

Mitch first heard of it when 'I got a phone call the next day early to say all hell had broken loose at the hotel in the early hours of the morning. Amy had run out of the room. She was covered in blood. Blake had scratches on his neck which were self-inflicted and Amy had to have a cut in her arm stitched, which she went to the hospital for and she ran away. She took a cab and he followed her and she finally went back. It was in the papers the next day. Photographs all over the papers ....'

'Did you think it was just a marital argument?' I ask him.

'... he had scratches on his neck. She kicked something. She had blood on her leg. Clearly there [was] a problem,' Mitch answers me.

'At that point I would not necessarily say it was a drug-induced problem. It was a problem. Even at that early stage I saw that this was a relationship, which [was] destructive .... I don't behave like that with my wife and most [people] don't ...'

☆ ☆ ☆

By the end of August, Blake's parents were talking to the press, commenting to the *People* and the BBC that both Blake and Amy needed help.

Giles even said that the couple were so close that if one died, the other might commit suicide. He added that he believed that both Amy and Blake thought they were in control of their drug habit but that wasn't the case. Both Georgette and Giles urged fans to boycott Amy's records to send a message.

Mitch, on the other hand, said publicly that he thought that wouldn't work and that both Amy and Blake would eventually reach rock bottom.

☆ ☆ ☆

I ask Mitch and Janis straight out if they believe Blake loves their daughter.

'No,' Janis says, 'it's his love for opportunity.'

'Very well put,' Mitch agrees. 'I don't think he loves her and I'll tell you why I don't think he loves her because if he loved her … he wouldn't say things like he did in the paper "I can't wait to see Amy because [I'm] going to pull her knickers down."'

Mitch says, 'That is not how I was brought up to talk. I was brought up to love and cherish my wife, both of them and I wouldn't talk like that in public about someone that I loved. He doesn't love her because if he did he wouldn't talk like that.'

'Does Amy find it disrespectful?' I ask him.

'She will excuse him,' Mitch replies. 'She would say that he didn't say it. That they made it up, but two newspapers independently said the same thing. It was in inverted commas, which means it is a quote and we all know he said it.'

'But [maybe],' I say, playing devil's advocate, '... in his terminology it's the way to say, "I love you."'

'Mmm ...', Mitch considers. 'How's this saying "I love you"? He called her a "crack whore". Is that a different way of saying I love you? It's the speak of somebody who's got no self-respect and no respect for his wife – somebody you should love and cherish. We've all done things to our wives we shouldn't have done – Janis and I are an example of that – but at no point have I shown her that disrespect and disregard. We all use different terminology, but this [shows] no respect for her; no respect for himself ...

'No, he doesn't love her.'

alcoholic logic

'Does Amy want to live?', I ask Mitch.

'To live? I think so,' he says. 'Nobody I have spoken to regarding her situation tells me that she is suicidal. She is always planning for the future.'

So what is she doing then? I ask Mitch about this.

'There are people that take drugs that are not suicidal,' he replies. '... There have been people who have taken drugs for 40 years – people who you and I wouldn't realize are taking drugs.'

'Does she realize what she is doing?' I say.

'I don't think she does.'

'It must be the most frustrating position to be in your shoes,' I comment. 'You do realize what she is doing. You have a beautiful talented girl who is killing herself – [was] probably from the time we ... started this interview. She is killing herself at this moment and it must be so frustrating for you.'

☆ ☆ ☆

After the Sanderson incident, all eyes were focussed on Amy, whose life was seemingly being played out in the public eye like a very tragic drama. Everyone had an opinion on Amy – her music; her marriage; her addictions; her behaviour. Friends and family urged Amy to go back into rehab. In late August 2007, however, several papers reported that Amy had claimed that Blake would commit suicide if she left him alone to return there.

Amy's mother, Janis, gave an interview to *First* magazine, in which she talked about Amy's problems. She said, 'I knew she was smoking marijuana but not that she was doing class A drugs until she collapsed. She won't stop until she sees the point of stopping … when I saw her afterwards, I did not tell her to clean up. There was no point.'

This attitude fits in with what Janis repeatedly tells me in our various discussions – it's 'tough love' – 'I cannot help you unless you help yourself'. But without a doubt, someone needs to help save Amy. And if it is not her mother, then who else is there?

☆ ☆ ☆

'Looking back … is there a moment when you think that either you or Mitch could have done something different?' I ask Janis.

'No!' she says coldly. '… I am a believer … that we live the life that has been dealt to us. … because that is what makes us, *us*. … Amy's experience of fame is like … "Wow!

Could it be possible? Could *I* really, really be like that."
And, [I think] ... scared her.'

Dealing with success can be very scary, I comment,
especially if you're constantly questioning if it will
continue.

Janis agrees, 'I think it is all about maturity.' She adds
that Amy is childish.

'Her songs are very mature, but she is very childish, like
"I don't want to be a woman. ...''', I respond, adding,
'I understand that she doesn't even have periods? Like
many anorexics.'

'Yes,' Janis agrees, 'but she has said that she has [had
periods] recently. It is hard to know where Amy is coming
from, because what she says is, "Mum, don't worry. I have
got this in hand and I have got that in hand". [But] Alex
will say, "Mum, she is not telling the truth."'

'But do you *know* she is not telling the truth?' I say.

'... Yes. She doesn't want me to be troubled by it because
I have got enough troubles. With Amy it is a case of we are
living in "Amyland". ... It is very surreal. I certainly feel
that way with her life. ... [W]hen people say "Wow! Are
you Amy's Mum" and I say "Yeah, [but] she is just a regular
person". *And she is.* Family and friends will say, "That is
Amy." There is no surprise ... she has always been that way.
It is a case of "... what's the fuss?" ... They know Amy.'

'It is one thing to be childish,' I comment, 'but hard
drugs are something else.'

'I think that is par for the course,' Janis replies. 'It is
almost as if I am living her past experience. Yes, she is on
the hard drugs. She is a Jazz Queen. She just does it all. ...
She would be upset if she thought I was upset.'

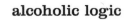

'So, she doesn't know that you and Mitch ARE upset?' I repeat.

'No.'

'She thinks that you are happy?' I persist.

'Yes,' she confirms. '[Amy] thinks that we are okay. … She doesn't know the pain that she is causing us. But being us, [we] don't want her to know of the pain we are experiencing, because we don't want to upset her. And that is parenting, God bless it.'

'It is very tricky being a parent', I comment.

'I couldn't be taught it,' Janis agrees. 'I am the mother that I didn't have and would have liked,' she adds.

This comment from Janis really strikes me as very interesting. In my experience, any parent who is asked if he or she has been a good father or a good mother, would, of course, like to respond 'Yes', but that person would also usually have some doubts (whether vocalized, or not) about that.

With Janis though, there is no doubt in her mind. She is a great mother. And while, in many ways, I'm sure that she is a very good mother to her children, her lack of any doubt is, I have to say, in my experience quite unusual.

☆ ☆ ☆

As most of the media focussed on Amy's problems, others, perhaps surprisingly, ignored them, stressing instead Amy's edgy rock chick style. A source was reported to have told the *Daily Mirror*, for example, that American *Vogue* editor Anna Wintour had cried 'get me Amy' for the cover of the September 2007 issue as the musician oozed cool. When that particular issue hit the newsstands, however, Sienna Miller graced its cover.

Despite all this, and even after further cancelled concerts, Amy's fans and many of her music peers made it clear that they still appreciated her talent. Amy received several nominations in 2007 for key music awards. Early in September of that year, she appeared at the Mercury Music Prize awards ceremony at London's Grosvenor House in Mayfair, giving, by all accounts, a breathtaking performance of 'Love Is A Losing Game', accompanied by just an acoustic guitar. Nominated for the award, along with the likes of the Arctic Monkeys, Bat For Lashes and Dizzee Rascal, Amy lost to the Klaxons. Afterwards she announced to a London evening paper that she was well after her holiday with Blake and couldn't see what all the fuss had been about.

A few weeks later, on 19 September, she appeared at the MOBO (Music of Black Origin) Awards at the 02 Arena in London's Greenwich. This time nominated for several awards, including Best R&B, Best Song ('Rehab') and Best Video ('Back To Black'), Amy won the Best UK Female award. She also performed at the awards. Looking painfully thin, a seemingly distracted Amy sang out of time and stared into space, as she performed 'Me and Mr Jones' and 'Tears Dry On Their Own', an appearance for which she was subsequently panned in the press.

Although Amy was reported to be on a downward cycle, she was still winning awards for her talent. On 8 October 2007, she won the Best Album award at the Q Awards. Mark Ronson picked it up on her behalf, but during the

partying afterwards ended up misplacing it. The slightly
bemused general manager of Bar Soho, a Central London
bar, subsequently discovered it in the venue's toilets.

In October, Ronson released a cover, with Amy on
vocals, of the Zutons' song 'Valerie' from his album *Version*.
The single shot to No. 2 in the UK single charts. Otherwise,
however, Amy wasn't doing so well. On a tour of Europe,
Amy played Germany and Denmark, before performing in
Norway, where she and Blake were arrested in Bergen on
18 October. According to reports, they were released the
next day, after being fined for possession of marijuana, after
which Amy continued her tour.

After Amy won the MTV Artists' Choice award in
November, one of the most coveted music awards, Island
released a deluxe version of *Back To Black* and a DVD called
'I Told You I Was Trouble: Live in London', which included
interviews with Amy, Island's Darcus Beese and Mitch
Winehouse, driving around in his taxicab. It also showed a
live performance at Shepherd's Bush earlier in the year.

But while Amy was winning awards, on a personal
front things were about to get much worse. Her
relationship with Blake was still up and down and Blake
had an assault charge hanging over his head from an
alleged encounter with a barman in Hoxton, East London,
in June 2006.

☆ ☆ ☆

Mitch says of that time, 'Amy and Blake's relationship was
very much up and down ... and we knew ... [that] he
[Blake] had a serious criminal case pending ...

'He [had] assaulted somebody or allegedly assaulted somebody and he knew he had this hanging over his head and he knew they would have this court case [going] on for sometime. This is *all* we knew. We didn't know *anything* about anything else, and Amy and I were talking about [it]. He felt that he might go to prison for a considerable amount of time and I would sit and talk to them about what we would do ... you know, how we could resolve the problems and everything else. But basically there was not an awful lot we could do. Because we knew at some point he would have to face the consequences of his actions. And he had a date to appear in court and it was cancelled and he had another date and it was cancelled and ... while all this [was] going on, there [were] problems occurring of varying degrees – Amy giving performances that weren't great ... Amy doing great performances but ... you know it was inconsistent.'

☆ ☆ ☆

On 9 November 2007, Amy's 'Baby', Blake, was arrested. Photographs of a tearful Amy kissing a handcuffed Blake appeared on the front pages of many newspapers. Blake, it seemed, was being charged with perverting the course of justice by attempting to fix the outcome of a trial.

After receiving a tip-off and secretly filming some meetings at which Blake was reported to be present, *the Daily Mirror* alerted the police that Blake and his friend Michael Brown, both accused of assaulting a barman, were allegedly trying to pay the victim £200,000 to drop the charges and were planning to whisk him out of the country so that their case would be dropped. Police subsequently raided Amy and Blake's home in Camden, using a battering ram to knock down the door, but the couple weren't there. Blake's arrest took place later at a flat in Bow, East London.

A distraught Amy later tried to visit her husband, only to be turned away, as Blake's mother had already been to see her son and prisoners were only allowed one visitor a week.

Friends and family worried about how Amy would react without Blake at her side with all the media attention she was receiving, but Amy, perhaps surprisingly, decided to carry on with her biggest British tour. The opening night on 14 November 2007, however, at the NIA venue in Birmingham was a shambles, ending with Amy being booed by loyal fans among the 13,000-strong crowd. She responded by telling them to wait until Blake got out of 'incarceration'. She eventually walked off stage halfway through a performance of 'Valerie'. Her spokesman later explained that Amy had had a particularly bad day after visiting Blake for the first time at Pentonville Prison in North London.

As if it could not get worse, Amy's tour manager, Thom Stone, later resigned during the Glasgow leg of the tour; stories began to circulate that he had had enough after heroin that he had 'passively inhaled' while on Amy's tour bus was found in his system.

A UN senior official also accused both Amy and model Kate Moss of glamorizing cocaine use, which could, he said, in turn, lead to Colombian drug barons carving more of a path into Europe's cities and causing devastation to parts of Africa. Around the same time, a video appeared on YouTube of a gig in Zurich, in which Amy was accused of allegedly retrieving drugs from her beehive. It was later claimed that the singer had just pulled out a tissue to wipe her nose, which she stuffed up her sleeve afterwards.

Amy played a show at Newcastle Academy on 18 November 2007 and got fantastic reviews, but further scandal broke when she was allegedly photographed after a gig in Blackpool on 20 November with white powder visible in her right nostril, leading to such headlines as 'Winehouse goes back to white' from the *Sun*.

Island released *Frank* for the first time in the States on that same date. It immediately went to No. 61 on the Billboard charts, showing that even a lot of bad press and a cancelled tour couldn't hurt Amy's sales over there. In England, Amy played just a few more dates, before cancelling her tour at the end of November.

She said in her statement, 'I can't give it my all on stage without my Blake … My husband is everything to me.'

Her label insisted that the cancellation had nothing to do with Amy's alleged drug problems but that the touring and the emotional toll of recent weeks had meant that Amy had to take a complete rest to deal with 'health issues'.

☆ ☆ ☆

'You know where you go to Al Anon and … they say "My name is …?" Can you say, "My name is Janis Winehouse and my daughter is addicted?"' I ask Janis at our meeting at the London Intercontinental hotel in November 2008.

'No,' she replies. 'Because she [Amy] has to. It has to be ... [that she can] say "This is the problem that I have". ... She has not said to me ... "Can you help me?" She has never said that to me – and I have never pushed her to do anything, because it's got to be what Amy wants. And I respect that.'

I ask her how she thinks Amy will take that first step towards urgently needed recovery.

'... I don't know. It's something that Mitch and I talk about all of the time. It has to be that Amy has to acknowledge that. And it's a bit like, you can't take a horse to water and make it drink. If it doesn't want to, it won't.

'... As a mother I'm there for my baby ... Amy says she's an addicted personality ...'

'She says, "*She's* an addicted personality"? I repeat.

'Yes. Yes.'

'But she doesn't at this moment see it as a problem? What she's addicted to?' I am trying to understand Janis's perspective on this.

'... She doesn't say anything about anything.'

I can't help but wonder why Janis doesn't push Amy further to discuss such key issues with her. When talking to Janis, I have the strong impression that she would love to have closer and better communication with Amy, but as Janis is not able to be with her daughter all the time, like Mitch, she doesn't know how to create a more intimate mother-daughter relationship. I think that Janis would be very happy if Amy would open up to her but she doesn't know how to ask the questions – she is scared of being rejected by her daughter.

☆ ☆ ☆

Further reports of Amy's erratic behaviour were printed in the press, particularly one photograph of Amy stumbling around the streets of East London at 5.40 a.m. in freezing temperatures, dressed in just a red bra and jeans, that was printed in most papers in Britain; the story even made the *New York Post*. But still the accolades for Amy's talent kept coming, never more so than when she received six Grammy nominations (for Best New Artist, Record and Song of the Year for 'Rehab', Best Pop Vocal Album, Best Female Pop Vocal Performance, and Album of the Year for *Back To Black*) competing against such artists as Kanye West and Beyoncé.

A distressed Janis had seemingly had enough though. In an Open Letter to her daughter, which was published in the British Sunday paper the *News of the World* on 9 December 2007, Janis begged Amy to seek help. She wrote that the letter was her way of making sure that Amy knew that all she needed to do was 'take the first step' and tell Janis what was troubling her and then Amy's family would help her. She commented that Amy had always been as 'stubborn as a mule' and that early fame had dizzied her, muddled her mind, but that she was just an ordinary human being, 'no stronger' than any of the rest of them.

She added that Amy thought that she could get through her problems by herself but she couldn't, and if she came to Janis first, Amy's family could help her. She wrote, 'You are still my baby' and 'I want you back'. She also stated in the letter that Amy was a brilliant talent and if she got herself well enough again, she would go on to fulfil her destiny.

It's not only Janis who has attempted to communicate with Amy through the *News of the World* – both Blake and his mother, Georgette, have spoken to the paper. Blake used his interview in November 2008 as a tool to reach out to Amy – and he knew exactly which buttons to push. Blake said all the right things, claiming that he introduced Amy to hard drugs and that he was willing to leave her so that she would recover from her addictions.

Mitch, too, says very intimate things about his daughter to the media – he even wants to tell me details about Amy's periods. It does make me wonder how Amy feels about this. If my mother or father or boyfriend sold a story about my private life to the press, I would be devastated. It would seem like such an invasion of privacy. I feel a lot of sympathy for Amy. But it seems to me that newspapers and the media play a special role in the Winehouse family's daily life and also in their communication with each other. In a way, I think this family feels that if it airs its problems in public, then at least it puts everything on the record. This certainly seems to create a lot of emotion within the family – but for them, it's just quite natural.

☆ ☆ ☆

'If I were to ask you to put the Amy Winehouse story into one sentence [what would that be]?' I ask Janis.

'It would be Amy Winehouse, living life to the edge,' she replies.

'That *is* scary,' I comment.

'Yes,' she agrees, 'but that is what she does. Always. Always.'

'Does she do it intentionally or … subconsciously?' I say.

'… I don't know … she just does [it].'

'When I am listening to you,' I continue, '… I am very intrigued. What I hear from the Amy Winehouse story is that she is from a very loving, united family but very lonely people. She is lonely; you are lonely. Basically [are you] very lonely people looking for love?'

'Yes!' Janis agrees. 'We are unfulfilled and we are seeking the fulfilment.'

'What is the one sentence, the one line from Amy's songs that you think is about you?' I say.

'It is the one "I can't help you, if you don't help yourself."'[1]

I ask if she repeated this back to Amy when she was in trouble.

'No,' Janis tells me but she adds, 'It is always there at the back of my mind. … I can't help her if she doesn't help herself. And, … that is Amy. … [She] is in denial all the time.

'"Oh Mum,"' Janis says, putting on her daughter's voice. '"I am okay. Don't worry. Don't worry."'

☆ ☆ ☆

After Blake's arrest, Amy moved out of their home in Camden to Bow in East London. The world's media seemed to camp outside her door, catching Amy's every move and encounter on camera. Friends alleged that Amy's house move was prompted by her wanting to get away

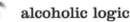

from the bad memories of her overdose and Blake's arrest, which were associated with the Camden house she had shared with her husband.

Others, however, were quick to comment on Amy's choice of company, such as musician Pete Doherty, who himself reportedly had a drug problem, and reports emerged that Amy's behaviour was getting worse, if anything. Blake's mother is alleged to have stated that Amy was taking more drugs than ever.

Amy seemingly told friends that if she didn't deal with her problems over Christmas she would check into rehab in the New Year. She spent the holiday period in the Caribbean with friends and a newly blonde Amy was seen in London in early January 2008.

In the end, however, it seemed that matters were perhaps taken out of her hands when a video was posted on the web of Amy allegedly smoking crack cocaine at a party at her home in Bow. In the *Daily Mail*, Mitch said that the video 'may well be the best thing that has ever happened to her … it may finally be the thing to focus her mind and convince her to get the help she needs to quit for good'.

On 24 January 2008, Amy, accompanied by her friend Kelly Osbourne and Mitch, checked into a rehab facility, the Capio Nightingale Hospital, near Marylebone, London. Universal released a statement saying that after talks with her label, management, family and doctors, Amy had come to realize that she needed 'specialist treatment to continue her ongoing recovery from drug addiction'.

The move, while hailed by many Winehouse fans, also brought much speculation about whether Amy would attend the Grammys.

Sure enough in early February 2008, the BBC, among others, reported that Amy's application for a US visa had been declined. A spokesman for Amy commented that she was disappointed but was concentrating on her recovery. At the final hour, the US embassy reversed its decision, but Amy was now set to appear in front of a select audience made up mostly of family and friends at the Riverside Studios in West London.

Her performance was to be broadcast live via satellite to the awards, a decision that she stuck to, singing 'Rehab' and 'You Know I'm No Good' to a standing ovation from the LA audience. The Grammys were a huge success for Amy, who picked up five of her six awards (Herbie Hancock picked up the Album of the Year for *River: The Joni Letters*).

A visibly shocked Amy thanked Island Records, her parents and Blake, her incarcerated husband – and, also, London because 'Camden Town is burning down', a reference to the fire that was destroying large parts of the area where she and Blake had lived.

Afterwards, Amy returned to the Capio Nightingale hospital and rehab.

☆ ☆ ☆

'Do you think Amy knows how much you love her?' I ask Janis and Mitch. 'She cries out for more attention [from you]. She basically takes all your attention.'

'I think that is possible,' Janis replies. 'That is what she does. The thing is, it is there for her. It is unconditional.'

'But does she know [that]?'

'It is funny you should say that … Maybe it is Amy's way of attention seeking,' Mitch says.

'It is like saying "Hey guys! Me! Me! Me!"' I throw up my hand.

'Well …' Mitch responds. 'She *has* got our attention.'

'As a parent … do you have your moments when you say "What have I done – what *did* I do wrong?"' I ask them both.

'No! No! No!!!' Janis says emphatically. 'I don't go down that road. … You have just got to … move on. [There] is no question of "It is my fault that this happened" and looking for [someone to] blame. That is a guilt thing. *No. No.* Everything I have done it was all in place.'

'You have been a good mum?' I ask Janis.

'Yes!' she replies without any hesitation whatsoever.

'She is a wonderful mother,' Mitch interjects, although it is my perception that he is saying this because he left Janis alone with the kids when he married Jane. Mitch had been conducting his affair with Jane for years and so even before he left, he was only half there for Janis. So I think he wants to jump in to say that Janis is a wonderful mother – it's the gentlemanly thing to do and, of course, it eases his guilt.

'I have *no* doubt about *that*,' Janis continues.

'Have you asked Amy … "Why? What are you missing? What is going on?"' I query.

'No. Because … as far as I am concerned [Amy] always says, "Mum, don't worry, everything is okay. Don't worry." She doesn't want to worry me,' Janis ends simply.

'But she does [make you worry …]?' I query.

'Yes,' Janis agrees. 'But … what do you do? As a parent, you are a parent and you cannot change the nature of that.'

'I know spending a lot of time with Mitch right now that he is actually 24–7 worrying about Amy. The phone is ringing and it's … "Oh, my god!" Or [if] it doesn't ring, [it's] "What is happening?"' I comment to Janis. 'How much Amy-time do you have a day? Not just like spending time with her – but *worrying* about her?'

'I think it is hard to put it actually into time,' Janis replies. '… It is like life. … There is a part of me that says, "No … I know that Amy is going to be all right."'

'… Do you know how difficult it is to overcome addiction?' I ask Janis.

'Oh, yes.'

'It [takes] a huge strong will,' I continue. 'Do you think she has a strong [enough] will to get well?'

'I don't know,' Janis replies. 'That is a tough one …'

Mitch interrupts, 'She *has* got a tremendous strong will.'

'To cure herself?' I question.

'Absolutely? I do believe that in six months, a year, two years ….' But then – after facing my questioning – he adds, 'She will always be a recovering addict. There is no such thing as anybody who is cured.'

☆ ☆ ☆

After a short time in rehab, Amy discharged herself, this time appearing days later at the BRIT Awards, where she performed with Mark Ronson and mouthed 'I love you' at the camera to Blake who was still on remand awaiting sentence.

It would not be long before the papers were again speculating about Amy's mental and physical health and her marriage when it was reported that she had shared a hotel room with artist Blake Wood, or 'Good Blake' as the media referred to him, after the BRITS. Amy also appeared to have scratches on her arms, fuelling speculation that she was self-harming again.

Professionally though, Amy seemed to be doing well: rumours abounded that she was set to start work on her next album (subsequently quashed when Amy reportedly delayed the recording sessions that Island Records had arranged for her in the Bahamas) and she also found herself nominated for three Ivor Novello songwriting awards.

But, on a personal front, Amy was reported to be again spiralling out of control. In April, she was cautioned by police after going an a drink-fuelled bender that involved her slapping a man, kissing another one and then reportedly openly smoking drugs in the street. A few days later, ending the apparent '96 hours of carnage' she was again in the papers, this time for having allegedly cheated on Blake with 'good boy' Alex Haynes and telling friends that her marriage to Blake was over.

By May, however, Mark Ronson, who had been working with Amy on the theme tune to the latest James Bond movie, an honour for any musician, had cancelled their recording sessions, leading to rumours that that the couple had argued over Amy's fitness to record.

Over the next months, Amy's very public deterioration was tracked in the press. After reports that Amy had collapsed again in June 2008, Mitch claimed that his daughter had been diagnosed with emphysema and that if she went back to smoking drugs it wouldn't just ruin her voice but would kill her. But just days later, a very frail looking Amy was present at Nelson Mandela's 90th birthday celebration in Hyde Park, a performance that attracted a lot of attention when she changed the words of the Specials' 1984 song 'Free Nelson Mandela' to 'Free-ee Blakey My Fella'.

In July, Blake who was formally charged with perverting the course of justice and grievous bodily harm, was sentenced to 27 months in prison, nine of which he had already served. He was expected to be released by the end of the year. Amy wasn't present at his sentencing.

After an alleged 36-hour bender in July 2008, involving what one newspaper later called 'an inhuman amount of hash' Amy was hospitalized, having reportedly overdosed for a second time. This led to concerns over her mental health – some journalists even suggested that she had shown symptoms of schizophrenia and others that she might have suffered brain damage as a result of her two overdoses.

☆ ☆ ☆

It was after this that Mitch first contacted me. At that time, I didn't really know that much about Amy Winehouse. My friends Gary Thompson of News International and Simon Bucks of SKY News kept pushing me to pursue the story of 'Amy's addictions'. But it was only after my initial meetings with Mitch in London at *Les Ambassadeurs* and the Intercontinental hotel, when we began to speak properly about what it was like to fight his daughter's addictions, that I really felt that, although Amy was not as big in America as she was in UK, there was something more to the story. But I had no clue how much 'more'.

In November 2008, at the second of these meetings, we discussed some of my most famous television specials with Michael Jackson's parents during his sensational trial. The first, I produced with Liz Murdoch and aired just after his arrest. The second aired on the eve of the beginning of Michael's trial.

It occurred to me, while speaking to Mitch, that he and Janis face many of the same questions that Joe and Katherine Jackson had to answer to during their son's trial. All of them have been or are being publicly judged as parents; they also have in common the loneliness that comes from being unable to share their concerns about their children without feeling the embarrassment or the condemnation of strangers. And there is also perhaps the same public perception of the Winehouses that, like the Jacksons, they have allegedly made money out of their child's talent.

In these early encounters, I find Mitch articulate, warm and sometimes painfully candid, even tearful, when he discusses Amy and addiction. We cover a lot of ground and I am still thinking about whether I want to pursue this further when he utters the words that make my decision. *'If I can share what I have gone through and what I know by now and help one family at least, this is what I would like to do'.*

He wins me over. We schedule filming.

☆ ☆ ☆

November is a busy month. Blake Fielder-Civil is released from prison, having agreed to go to rehab. Amy isn't there to meet her husband, having just got out of the London Clinic herself, where she was being treated for a suspected lung infection. We are already filming with the Winehouses and they are spending nights in my London hotel. We are sort of 'living together'.

☆ ☆ ☆

Initially filming is just with Mitch, who talks about his upbringing, his family, his marriages and, of course, Amy and Alex, some of which I have already written about. But it is also essential that I speak with the rest of the family, particularly Janis, Jane and Amy, herself, the three women in Mitch's life. Without them a lot of the story will be lost.

I meet Jane, Mitch's second wife, just before we start filming in November, when Mitch brings her to dinner. Jane was his secretary and they had been having an affair for a long time before Mitch made the decision to leave Janis, Amy and Alex to be with her.

What strikes me first is that Jane is a very pleasant woman; she is also good looking, intelligent and hard working. She is Mitch Winehouse's wife now, but it becomes clear that when Mitch is there he wants to be in control. To make a point Jane almost has to announce that she's about to say something: *'Hey! I need to speak right now! I want to be involved.'*

I also noticed this very quickly when I was injured in an accident at the beginning of 2009 and Mitch and Jane were among the many guests who visited me at my vacation home. My heart immediately went out to Jane: the pair of them sat on my sofa but while Mitch talked constantly, Jane struggled to get involved in the

conversation. 'I want to be a part of it,' Jane said, when we discussed building a website to offer advice for families dealing with addiction and also creating a documentary that would try to deal with the subject of addictions.

Jane is supposed to be Mitch's 'First Lady', but it is clear that is not happening because Amy needs him constantly. In a way, I guess you could say, that is Amy's revenge. And then there is Janis, with whom Mitch still has a close relationship.

Of course, they're not the only family in the situation of having had a father leave his wife and children after having an affair, but their subsequent relationships *are* unusual because of Amy's problems. Mitch and Janis are still so involved with each other because of their daughter. Trying to save Amy also brings Janis and Jane together on a regular basis. I understand how strange it must be for Janis to have to collaborate with the woman whom Mitch left her for. Equally Jane must also feel awkward because, as Janis loves to point out, as long as Amy is sick, it will always be her and Mitch primarily dealing with it.

The dynamics between these two women and Amy herself are even more complicated. It seems to me that Amy does try to have a relationship with her mother and her step-mother but Mitch always needs to be in control and consequently all these relationships are monitored through him. Mitch is basically the centre point and I'm sure that playing that role is tough for him. Mitch often complains that it tears him into pieces, but I can't help but feel that he has created this situation and in a way it works for him because it enables him to have full control.

☆ ☆ ☆

My television crew are ultra-accommodating when it comes to filming Janis at the Intercontinental Hotel in London. She walks with a cane, visibly limping when she arrives, wearing simple slacks and a blouse. She looks very much like her daughter and is a vibrant, energetic woman. She is also very sexual. Very aware of herself, of her large breasts, about which she makes jokes all the time.

In our first interview, it becomes obvious that she is much tougher than Mitch, possibly much colder, in her attitude towards her daughter and her problem. While Mitch is trying to break through a wall to save Amy, Janis's attitude seems very much: *'What can I do? She has to come to a decision herself that she is addicted? What can I do?'* Her attitude towards Blake is very defined – to her he is nothing.

☆ ☆ ☆

I ask Janis what the most difficult moment was for her in the last few years. '... It looks like you think things turned really black for you when she married Blake,' I comment.

'Yes,' she agrees, 'but I believe [Amy] had to have been out of her head to do it.'

'Well,' I say, 'talking objectively what do you think she found in Blake?'

'I think she saw a chance to "rescue" him,' Janis replies, rolling her eyes dramatically, 'because she speaks of him as having [had] a terrible life. She says ... he didn't know what else to do and "I can help him" and it's ... that naivety

... that she can help people. That's what she wants to do all the time.'

'What's a day in the life of Amy like?' I ask.

"Well, she's not recording at the moment ...' Janis muses.

'She hasn't recorded since she met Blake, right?' I ask.

'Well, no, but she needs to get back ... [to] it. I think Amy is banging around not knowing what to do with herself.'

If she wants to record, though, what's stopping her, I say to Janis.

'I don't know,' she replies. 'I think it's just [Amy] can't get herself together. When she has to be anywhere she will take *forever* to get ready. ... She's not a person to rush and she has always taken her time.'

'I spoke to Mitch. ... He was heartbroken that he had to write a cheque for £100,000 for [Amy] missing a show in Paris.'

'Oh, yes.'

'And there was no explanation [for Amy's no-show]?' I query.

'No ... Mitch and I, thank God, are looking after her finances otherwise, my goodness, it would probably all be gone.'

'Mitch was telling me Blake has a very expensive drug habit something like £14,000 a week. ... Have you ever seen Amy ... on the hard drugs?'

'Well,' Janis replies, 'I've seen her where she can just about open her eyes and [is] really not with it.'

'That's really heartbreaking.'

'Yes, I want to say to her *"Amy, what are you doing? Don't you know what you're doing?"* But she has ... got herself onto it to help her get through. And I understand that.'

'What do you mean by that?' I ask, wanting to hear the answer.

'Well, she's finding life to be tough at the moment. And you would think she's got it all but she hasn't. She's … alone.'

'She's lonely?' I query. '… She has you, but …'

'Yeah, but what she needs is somebody who will love her … care for her … look after her on a one-to-one level because she hasn't got that,' Janis says.

'Does Blake love her?' I ask.

'I think they are playing the love game,' Janis responds. 'It's not true love. He's not being loving towards her. …'

'Do you think Amy understands that she is not loved by him?' I push.

'I think what's happening is with his using emotional blackmail it's … "if you loved me, you'd do such and such" [and Amy's] "Well, of course, I love you, of course I do." And he's playing a game with her.'

'What's their age difference?' I ask.

'A year.'

'But she's childish?'

'Yes. But the fact that he is the supplier of the drugs [means] he has the control,' Janis says.

'Did she know he was on hard drugs when she met him?' I ask.

'She forgave him for it,' Janis explains. 'And excused it by saying "Oh, he's had [a] hard life."'

'But Amy's intelligent – from a "good family"?' I say, meaning surely she should know better? She knows that hard drugs won't simply go away, especially as her mother is a pharmacist.

'She had always said, "They are not for me … I don't need them,"' Janis confirms. 'And probably the marijuana was as hard as it got [before]. … I think it's a case of [Blake] may have said "Try a bit of this. It'll make you really feel better." … I think that's how it began … He said, "No, really … I promise you it's good!"'

'When you saw Blake the first time did you think there was something wrong despite the fact that you didn't like him?'

'No!' she exclaims. 'I thought he was a *nothing*! That Amy had taken pity on him.'

'… When there was the problem,' I ask, 'did you think maybe I should call [his parents]?'

'No, no, no! Oh no!' Janis stresses emphatically. '… I had assessed [Blake's mother] quite quickly. I realized she … was trying to identify with Amy and Blake … "Oh I'm a youngster too!"' she mimics. '*No. She's. Not.*'

'… Are they still in good communication with Amy?' I enquire.

'*No*! Not at all. … They have not made any effort to contact Amy,' Janis states.

'Are they in good communication with their son?' I query.

'That I don't know,' Janis replies, continuing, '… but when I was abroad in Italy, Blake was with Amy and Blake called me "Mummy" – and it was as if he had stuck a knife in my belly. … I felt sick. How dare he call me "Mummy"?! *Who's he*?'

'What did you say?' I query.

'I said nothing! I think I probably went silent at that point,' she adds.

I ask her what she would do if Blake were here. 'Would you accept him in your house?'

'No! No! No!' she says definitely.

'If Amy wanted to bring him?' I persist.

'I'd say "Could you leave him at home?"'

'Where is home for him?' I say.

'In Camden.'

'Oh, with Amy?' I query.

'Well, yes. Or he's somewhere else. ... It's not a situation where she's been going out with him and I got to know him because I [didn't].'

'You just met him once before?' I ask and when Janis nods, add, 'Well maybe you and I are missing something about him.'

'I wonder about that. When he was on tour with her, he just followed her around like a lapdog and he did nothing. NOTHING! He was just there ... she went somewhere and he went there. And he did nothing and he's earned his nobody position by being a NOBODY.'

'Do you think Amy has the chance to recover if she remains with him?' I ask Janis seriously.

'No, ... because he will try to maintain control.'

'... And, if Amy wants £20,000 for drugs tomorrow?' I ask. 'What happens then. You cannot stop her?'

'No,' Janis replies. 'No. Because it's her money.'

☆ ☆ ☆

'What will happen if they don't divorce?' I ask Janis.

'They will kill each other,' she replies. '... Mitchell was saying before they arrested him they were not getting on.

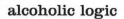

They were fighting all the time and Mitchell thinks they would have divorced earlier if he had not been arrested.'

'But would he be willing to divorce?' I query.

'That I don't know … The problem is he gives nothing to it except drugs.'

'Does she realize it?'

'Well … not yet.'

'So if there is no divorce, how are you going to prevent that?' I say.

'… I leave that with Mitchell, because Mitchell is doing all that needs to be done,' Janis says simply.

This is something that comes through strongly in my discussions with Janis. There is no doubt that she is a brave woman, coping with MS and trying to find a cure or a way to slow down the progression of the disease but, on the other hand, she is still the woman who was abandoned all those years ago by her husband for Jane, who is now his second wife. When it comes to Amy though, whether Jane or anyone else exists is largely irrelevant: it will always be in Janis's mind and speech 'Mitchell and I' dealing with their daughter Amy's problems. They are Amy's parents. And I think subconsciously – and I am not for a second saying that it is a conscious thought in Janis's mind – that it is very convenient for Janis that Amy is so sick and so self-destructive because 'Mitchell and I' will always take precedence over everything else. That relationship will always have top priority due to Amy's constant needs.

love is a losing game

'What is happening to my family and to Amy is going on throughout hundreds and thousands of homes, not just in this country but also around the world,' Mitch explains to me when I ask him to expand on why he feels this urgent need to help other families suffering addiction problems.

'The drug problem in this country is deep-rooted. I suppose it is deep-rooted throughout the world. We are in a fortunate position because we can go and speak to people and we can get the best advice and we can get the best help. There are hundreds and thousands of people who can't do that. What we want to do, and what I want to do, is to be able to help people in a position similar to my own, so that we can – perhaps through a website or through a charity, we haven't decided yet – make counsellors, therapists, solicitors available to people who under normal circumstances wouldn't be able to afford to go and see these people. That is how I feel. That is how we could put something back into society.

'I am very lucky in that I have got a very wonderful and understanding wife. I have got a wonderful and understanding ex-wife and I have got fantastic family and friends, so I never feel lonely in that respect ...'

He continues, 'Apart from professionals obviously, I am able to discuss things confidentially with my family and my friends and they are a great source of comfort to me.'

I ask him if he needed to research the effects of drugs.

He replies, 'Unfortunately, I have made a study of it and that's why this situation can't last forever. It has to ... eventually stop. That will be when Amy is ready to stop. ... I am ready for her to stop right now. I was ready for her to stop two years ago. It is not when I am ready; it is when she is ready. One of the other things, Daphne ... that I want to get across to people in a similar situation to me ... [is] it is not their fault. As long as they have tried to bring their children up the best way that they can ...

'... And another important message to get across is to carry on with your life. The worst thing is ... I have done that, is to stop and just sit in a room and cry all day. Nobody wants that. I don't want that. I have got a family that needs me and I want people to understand that they can carry on with their lives as they did before. Nobody has died.' I look at Mitch questioningly here and he repeats, 'Nobody is dead.'

'But you have not been able to have a normal life, a normal job. ... It is very difficult for you as well,' I comment.

'It is difficult but we manage to cope with it,' he says. 'It is stressful.'

'So', I ask. 'What was the most difficult day for you and Amy?'

'The most difficult day, I think was ... in about April 2008 ... [and] I am not telling stories out of school; it has been documented. She told Blake that she had been unfaithful to him and she really went into – she really was in a very, very bad situation. She cut herself and she was upset and Blake was upset and he had every right to be ... and she was in a very bad situation.

'She was in a recording studio ... in Henley, which is in Oxford, and I went down there and it was at that point that I tried to have her sectioned. To protect her. She had an episode which had been going on for a few hours. ... What people don't understand about sectioning is people are ... detained for their own safety and for the safety of other people, but to do that you have to have a GP, the Clinical Psychologist and the Local Area Health Authority [representative there] and by the time those three people [usually] convene the episode is over.

'So, in other words, it is very, very rare that anybody is sectioned because by the time they get there it is finished, and that is exactly what happened with Amy. When the doctor got there ... it had passed and she was back to "relative normality".

'And what we found out at that point is [that] the only person who can request a mental health assessment is the next of kin – and the next of kin is Blake. I am not saying that Blake wouldn't want to protect her but because he was in prison at the time it was just an impossibility anyway. Having said that, had she been psychotic and really a threat to herself and anyone else, they would have dealt with it, but to request a mental health assessment [requires] the next of kin and that was the worst situation ever.'

'What was worse, to call the doctor or to initiate it?' I ask.

'... To initiate it and to think that my child could be taken away,' Mitch replies. 'I wanted her to be taken away to protect her. She wasn't suicidal but she was clearly unwell and that is what I feel is wrong with the laws in this country ... you read about it all the time where somebody should have been detained under the Mental Health Act and they have pushed somebody under a train. ... or they have stabbed somebody. They should have been detained under the Mental Health Act, so these people are walking around, when for their own safety and the safety of others they should be detained.

'Amy isn't in that situation,' he clarifies. '... I have just given you an extreme example, and the laws in America aren't that much different. ... We are not trying to lock people away. We are trying to help them and even if somebody is ... sectioned, after 72 hours if they display any kind of improvement they are released. So, really, when you think about it and when you reflect upon it, there isn't really any way that somebody can be helped in this country unless ... they say "please help me."'

I ask, '[Isn't] that part of the treatment to say: "I am sick"?'

'That's right,' Mitch says. '... Amy has instigated a drug replacement programme and she has put on, since those horrible days, at least 20 pounds in weight and her drug consumption has greatly reduced, although there is the odd episode and there have been situations where she has had a seizure. ... [O]bviously it is very serious [but] it's not really as it was. Things have improved.'

I ask if this is because Blake has been in jail.

'I am not saying it is because he is in jail. What I am prepared to say is that since May ... her situation has generally improved. ...'

I say to Mitch, 'If I were Blake sitting here now, in one sentence what would you tell me?'

'Well what a good question. ... I would walk out! I really don't want to talk to him ... I wouldn't say anything. I have tried reasoning with him by doing all the normal things any normal person would do, and unfortunately it has fallen on deaf ears. Right now, especially after the last episode with him saying that he wants "to pull Amy's knickers down", I would get up and I would walk out.'

'And, what would you say to Amy?'

'I would tell her how much we love her. How much we will always love her. That is never going to change ... and how much we need her. How much she needs us. ... *I want my daughter to be a whole person again*. That is what I would say to her.'

'You are a good man,' I say quietly. Mitch is very receptive to such a simple comment. It is as if he needs to hear it again, so, I repeat, 'You are a very good man.'

☆ ☆ ☆

My television crew and I spend days filming with Mitch, and sometimes with Janis, in November. Mitch and Jane, a lovely woman who has to show so much understanding

about the constant attention Amy's situation demands, sometimes sleep over at my hotel.

Mitch does find it therapeutic to relive memories of his own childhood, his life with Janis and the children, the journey to Amy's stardom, and then dealing with Amy's problems, including having to face his daughter almost dying twice, and then trying to find the best possible way to save her. But between filming and dealing with Amy, pretty much around the clock, he is exhausted at night, so Mitch – and Jane sometimes – stay in London to spare them the drive back and forth from their home and also just to allow them to be in a different environment where Mitch, in particular, can relax.

It also means that Mitch can visit Amy, who is back in hospital at the London Clinic in Harley Street, not that far from my hotel in Park Lane. According to the media, Amy has had a bad reaction to the medication she has been taking as part of a drug replacement programme. Rumours also abound that Amy and Blake's marriage is over as Amy has not visited him in rehab. Mitch is very worried and is also having to cope with drug dealers who are apparently trying to smuggle drugs into Amy, even though there is a security team in place.

Mitch says he needs to get the word out to them that there is no money for drugs, and perhaps they will go away.

One evening in early December, my producer, Erbil, and I decide to have dinner with my close friends Bitu Bhalla, his wife Karen and their children at their home in Richmond. I have known Bitu since December 2007 when Asif Ali Zardari (now president of Pakistan), Benazir Bhutto's husband, introduced us, just two weeks before his

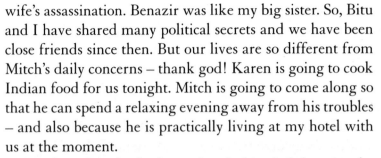

wife's assassination. Benazir was like my big sister. So, Bitu and I have shared many political secrets and we have been close friends since then. But our lives are so different from Mitch's daily concerns – thank god! Karen is going to cook Indian food for us tonight. Mitch is going to come along so that he can spend a relaxing evening away from his troubles – and also because he is practically living at my hotel with us at the moment.

Mitch comes back from Amy's hospital late in the afternoon. He is in a great mood after seeing his daughter and has already told me that she looks so well. 'She's had a haircut and, Daphne, she looks like Marilyn Monroe,' he tells me.

He picks up the phone to speak to Raye, Amy's manager. He says, 'Raye, I am just here with Daphne and I am telling her that I just saw Amy and she looks fantastic. ... Her skin is clean again. She has gained some weight. She looks so good! *She is talking again about recording music*!'

Mitch is so happy that he suggests we don't use my chauffeur to get to Richmond, but that he drives instead. 'I am a taxi driver after all!' he says.

Just before we leave he takes a phone call, after which he says, his voice heavy with sarcasm, 'My son-in-law – can you imagine – has failed his urine test in the rehab that we were paying £30,000 [for]. ... He is going back to jail and ... he will have to serve his full term.'

The fact that Amy is paying for Blake's rehab is not news to me as Janis alluded to it when we first met, saying that Amy hadn't wanted to pay for it but that Blake had called her and begged her to, telling her that if she loved him, she would do it.

Mitch has made it clear to me by now that he can't stand Blake and doesn't know how to get rid of him. Janis feels this more so, as is evident from our conversations. Mitch is also pleased as he tells us that Amy, who seems so well now, 'hasn't spoken to Blake in weeks,' so everything looks great.

Mitch promises us a grand tour of London as Erbil and I climb into the back of his cab. We listen as Mitch tells us, via a microphone in the front of the taxi, about his city, London. Mitch and Erbil share a particular interest in football, so he points out football stadiums on the drive to Richmond. We laugh a lot because, when Mitch isn't stressed, he is very good company and is very entertaining.

Just before we arrive at Bitu's home, Mitch's phone rings again. He answers it and changes visibly before our eyes; the relaxed, humorous man disappears. *'What do YOU mean? How can that be?! Who allowed HIM to do that? I don't understand!! How did that happen?'* he fires back at whoever he is talking to. He then breaks off, calling someone else. The whole thing is so intense.

'How did that happen?' he questions. *'When did that happen? So HE IS on the run. ...'*

He breaks off to say to us, 'You won't believe that Blake. ... When I told you that Blake ... was sent back from rehab to jail, apparently he didn't go ... He disappeared and he is on the run. And he surfaced in Amy's hospital ... so drunk and, after hours of taking drugs ... so out of it. And now they are together ... I am talking to security and they cannot stop him because he is her husband.'

But Blake is also on the run from the police and his arrival at Amy's hospital room is yet another problem that Mitch now has to deal with. While Mitch is trying to call

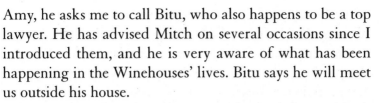

Amy, he asks me to call Bitu, who also happens to be a top lawyer. He has advised Mitch on several occasions since I introduced them, and he is very aware of what has been happening in the Winehouses' lives. Bitu says he will meet us outside his house.

By the time the cab pulls up outside Bitu's house, Mitch has called the security guard back: 'Where is he? How did it happen? Let me talk to Amy! Oh, they're in a closed room? OK, get Amy on the phone and call me back.'

Within two minutes he is speaking to his daughter. 'Amy,' Mitch says, 'put Blake on the phone. No! I will not yell at him. Just put him on the phone.'

I tell him: 'Mitch, collect yourself. Be calm.' And he follows my advice.

I am impressed that Mitch is handling the situation. He seems almost calm. Mitch tells his son-in-law, 'Listen Blake, you have to go and turn yourself into the authorities. We will take care of you. [But] you cannot stay with Amy right now. It is not good for Amy. [And], it is not good for you.'

Bitu is waiting for us, smoking a cigarette, as he watches us descend from the taxi. We discuss whether we should go to the hospital but we decide collectively that Mitch, while composed at the moment, might not be able to hold it together when he sees Blake and might make the situation worse. He also has Bitu to advise him and Bitu's two other guests are also top American lawyers.

Finally we find ourselves inside Bitu's home, with Bitu's wife, Karen and their two beaming kids all present – and they are all being very supportive of Mitch's predicament, even though it is interfering with our dinner plans. This is meant to be a relaxing evening and is our first family meal at the Bhalla home. It is also obvious that Karen has been cooking all afternoon, if not all day, for this meal.

Bitu and Mitch leave us to try to sort out the situation and are later joined by John Grimmer and Dan Paige, the two other lawyers, when they turn up.

Eventually Blake agrees to turn himself in, and it's only when Mitch is told this news that he starts to relax and the rest of us can really enjoy the evening. He even reaches the point where he can recount the evening's events with his unique brand of humour, making all of us, including John and Dan, who we give a lift to at the end of the night, scream with laughter at his stories.

When we get back to the hotel that night, Mitch says, 'I am exhausted.' I reply that I am exhausted, too, just from watching him. Mitch asks to stay over at my hotel. He seems so needy, so lonely that I say, 'Sure!'

But, in reality, this is his life. This is what saving Amy is all about — and this is part of the toll that it takes on everyone within her orbit.

☆ ☆ ☆

Just a few days later, however, Amy's behaviour seems to be deteriorating again and Mitch is very upset.

He tells us that the hospital and the doctors want to kick her out. She has been ordering champagne and not only drinking it herself but offering it to other patients in the hospital as well. It is completely ridiculous. He says that since Blake went there, it has all gone downhill.

While he is sitting with me, Mitch receives text messages from Blake and Blake's mother, Georgette, which make

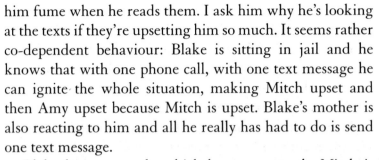

him fume when he reads them. I ask him why he's looking at the texts if they're upsetting him so much. It seems rather co-dependent behaviour: Blake is sitting in jail and he knows that with one phone call, with one text message he can ignite the whole situation, making Mitch upset and then Amy upset because Mitch is upset. Blake's mother is also reacting to him and all he really has had to do is send one text message.

Blake knows exactly which buttons to push. Mitch is very transparent, so it is quite easy for both Blake and Georgette to upset him.

There is clearly a war of words going on between Mitch and Blake. Mitch shows me a text that his son-in-law has sent, in which Blake has written:

I am not going to leave your daughter like you left her and her mother.

Mitch admits what is obvious – that Blake knows how to hit a nerve. He says 'He knows exactly how upsetting it is to me and how hurtful it is to Amy.'

'Well, if he knows how to push the right buttons and you know that he knows that … just ignore the messages.' I try to reason with him.

At this point Mitch shows me more messages from Blake, including one in which his son-in-law seems to suggest that he will be willing to go away if Mitch will just pay him a few months' rent on which to live. Mitch is prepared to do this just to get Blake out of his daughter's life.

The whole negotiation is taking place through text messages.

love is a losing game

I ask him what will happen if Amy and Blake do divorce and they still have the co-dependency issues that they appear to have. 'If they are drawn to each other [even] after their divorce,' I say to him, 'they can still see each other and still have the same horrible effect on each other.'

The 'divorce' only amounts to a piece of paper, after all.

Mitch is quiet as he hasn't thought about that question. His main concern at the moment is the drug dealers, who seem to be finding ever more inventive ways to get drugs to his daughter in hospital.

'There was a flower delivery,' he tells me, 'and it got me suspicious. I started to open the flowers and found a drug inside the leaves of the flowers.'

He tried hiring security to intimidate the dealers but Amy didn't warm to them, so he hired another team, but their job is to secure Amy, not to stop her from taking drugs or from drinking. Mitch has also tried to put it out that there is no cash for drugs, but his problem is his daughter. It is Amy's money, after all.

'She gave £7,000 in cash to somebody as a gift and she doesn't understand what it means,' he tells me, adding, 'I am trying to stop it but on the other hand, of course, it *is* her money. What can I do if she sends somebody to the bank? I am trying to be involved and make sure that … the bank … calls me. [But] if she really wants something, there is really nothing I can do.'

☆ ☆ ☆

I ask Janis, 'If there was a bottom line and you had a wish, what would it be?'

120

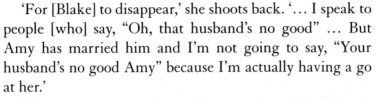

'For [Blake] to disappear,' she shoots back. '… I speak to people [who] say, "Oh, that husband's no good" … But Amy has married him and I'm not going to say, "Your husband's no good Amy" because I'm actually having a go at her.'

'Have you ever mentioned divorce to Amy?' I ask Janis. 'No, I haven't.'

Mitch says, 'Blake has. … I've got letters from Blake going back six months: "I wanna get a divorce, this situation is …" And every time he says it we say, "Can you confirm it, Blake. We'll send a solicitor in and confirm it." But he won't confirm it. Now I've got letters from Blake saying he doesn't want any money, he wants a divorce. … Although he has supposedly sent similar letters to Amy, I think she chooses to ignore them. She is living in a little bit of a fantasy world in regard to their relationship. And unless something drastic happens it won't be her that sorts a divorce [out].'

Mitch continues, '[Blake] asked me what he should do in terms of – this was since I've seen you – in terms of their relationship. … I was worried he might be taping the conversation. [I said] "I'm not telling you to do anything; however, every time you are on the phone to Amy she has a relapse. Every time you've been together with Amy since you've been married she's been in hospital six times and nearly died twice. She hasn't since you've been together made a recording and she's hardly performed and your plan is to come out and be with my daughter again – what do you think is going to happen Blake?"'

'And he said, "Well, I take your point."'

'I said, "At some point you're going to have to take responsibility for what happens to her in the future." And

he said, "Will you help me to get a flat and everything …"
I said, "… get your solicitor to confirm what the situation
is and we will discuss how we will help or if we will
help you."

"'First I've got to know if you're planning to go back to
Amy …" But I've told him whatever the situation [is] – and
even if I break the law – I cannot allow a situation similar
to that situation in the hotel where they nearly killed each
other … I've told him that if I have to break the door down
I'll break the door down. There won't be anything to stop
me getting to my daughter and helping her. You've got to
understand that!'

☆ ☆ ☆

'We have all got a very strong sense of family,' Mitch says.
'[Amy's] sense of family is even stronger, which is a kind of
contradiction and one of the "weapons" … it's not a nice
term, but one of the "weapons" I've used [to] distance
myself from her. Not distance myself from her emotionally,
but [I] don't see her as often and very, very quickly she will
say to Raye, her manager … "Where's my Dad? Is my Dad
OK? I haven't spoken to my Mum."

'I don't know if it does her any good. But I don't want
her to think because … I'll sit there and we'll have a
kiss and cuddle and have a cup of tea … that by doing this
I am in any way empowering her to carry on doing what's
she's doing.

'She knows what she is doing is not right … you know
we've talked about how close she was with my mother
[Cynthia]. All she's worried about is … she's very spiritual;

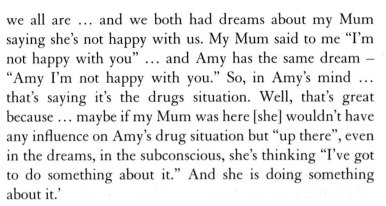

we all are … and we both had dreams about my Mum saying she's not happy with us. My Mum said to me "I'm not happy with you" … and Amy has the same dream – "Amy I'm not happy with you." So, in Amy's mind … that's saying it's the drugs situation. Well, that's great because … maybe if my Mum was here [she] wouldn't have any influence on Amy's drug situation but "up there", even in the dreams, in the subconscious, she's thinking "I've got to do something about it." And she is doing something about it.'

'… Amy talks about the future all of the time. She wants to move into her new home, she wants to put a studio in there and it's always, "Dad, can we do this? Dad, can we do that?" and "I'm really looking forward to going on tour in March 2009. Will you and Mum come with me." So when she's doing that she's talking about the future and how life is going to be in the future. … She does want to live.'

Janis interjects, 'But I think she probably feels trapped.'

'What do you mean?' I ask.

'Well, her body's trapping her with the addiction.'

☆ ☆ ☆

Janis and Mitch continue to visit their daughter in hospital. Janis tells me: '… When I saw her last night in the hospital and I held her hand when she was going to sleep I thought she is still my baby, and it reminded me of when I used to sit with her at night and read a story to her, and her brother as well … I could see that she looked like she was asleep so I let go of her hand and slipped away and she said "Mum

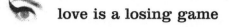

where are you?" and I said "Okay, I am here." ... That is what it was like – I had gone back in time to when she was a baby ... I could have picked her up in my arms and put her there like a baby, because that is how she is. It is like the need to rescue her is enormous; I just want her to be OK. I would do whatever it took to make that right and I am sure Mitch would as well. The pair of us are ... beside ourselves in what can we do to help her.'

'Can you do anything more than you already do?' I ask.

'I don't think so. I think we are doing everything that we can. It is a case of where she has to take herself to that edge and say, "Wow! Enough!"'

'And you just sit and wait?'

'Yes,' Janis replies.

I comment that this must be both painful and frustrating. Also, time is not on their side. Janis does not disagree.

'It is a case of there [are] times when control is not possible and you have just got to go with it. ... You have to go with the flow because that is all one can do. It's a tough one.'

☆ ☆ ☆

We have been filming for several weeks now and Mitch decides it is time to tell his friends and family about the documentary as it is starting to leak to the press. Amy is still in hospital, however.

I decide to host a party for him. The official reason for the celebration is that Mitch wants to wish his loved ones "Happy New Year" and he is also going to sing Sinatra.

The third reason, unbeknownst to Mitch is it's a surprise birthday party for him. The idea for the party first came up a few weeks earlier when I and my film crew went to a social club in Chiswick, where Mitch and his friend, Fred, performed from time to time. I initially thought we should have the party there, but Mitch said to me: *'No, no. Daphne, it is almost New Year. I want my family and friends to remember that night. Let's do it "Daphne style."'* It was important for him and so we did.

So, on a Friday evening in late December, *Les Ambassadeurs* in Mayfair is surrounded with extra security. Guests by invitation only – including the Winehouse extended family and close friends – pour into this exclusive venue via a separate entrance to attend a champagne reception. Every female guest will receive a yellow rose.

Sotiros, the manager of the club, renovates the basement quickly, just for this event. Within a few days, it becomes the glamorous 'Red Club'.

☆ ☆ ☆

In the days leading up to the party, though, I send my producer Erbil to Janis's house in North London to pick up some photographs. This is a trip down memory lane for him as he lived in West Finchley as a student, but he hasn't been back there in about 30 years.

When he arrives at the house someone lets him in. He immediately notices Janis standing in the kitchen doorway, using it to brace herself. She looks tired and needs to hold onto the frame for support. The hallway of the house is small, only wide enough for one person to navigate at a time – so perfect for Janis, but strange to someone used to the large box-like houses of the United States.

There are two tiny rooms to the left of the main hallway, and two larger rooms on the right-hand side. The first room on the right is Janis's bedroom, where they go first. Three photographs hang on the walls. One image of a mountain top immediately grabs Erbil's attention. He asks Janis what it is. The photograph is obviously important to her as it's quite prominently displayed.

Janis tells him that she went there with a group of family and friends. 'Of course Amy was not there!' she adds.

'Why not?' Erbil asks.

Janis responds, 'Why, if I had taken her there, she would have found a way to kill herself!'

Both Mitch and Janis have already told me how fatalistic Amy is and how she often plays on this to scare them, albeit probably to get their attention.

Now Janis recounts to Erbil how many times Amy has been near death – running into roads after dogs and so on. Amy was the kind of child that needed to be under constant surveillance in order to prevent her from harming herself, it seems.

The way that Janis describes her indicates to Erbil that Amy is pretty much still that same little kid.

After they leave the bedroom, Erbil helps Janis along the corridor where he comes across two men. The first is in his mid-50s and looks very tired. We later find out from Mitch that he is an old friend of Janis's, someone who sometimes helps her out. A much larger, burlier man turns out to be Janis's boyfriend. He disappears into one of the other rooms. The house is quite small and sombre.

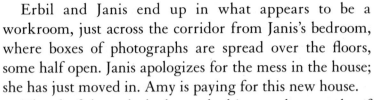
Erbil and Janis end up in what appears to be a workroom, just across the corridor from Janis's bedroom, where boxes of photographs are spread over the floors, some half open. Janis apologizes for the mess in the house; she has just moved in. Amy is paying for this new house.

They leaf through the boxes, looking at photographs of Amy, Janis, Mitch and Alex, as well as other members of the family, while Amy's cats crawl over Janis and the photographs. Janis is looking after them for her daughter as Amy is incapable of looking after them herself, she explains.

Erbil spends quite a long time with Janis in this room, looking at the photos, listening to her as she reminisces about Amy in a tender and loving manner, usual for a mother discussing her daughter.

He stays until he realizes that Janis is tired out, but he is concerned that she hasn't eaten and is hungry. It seems odd to him that there are two men in the house, capable of cooking or fetching something to eat, yet they seem to him to be waiting for Janis to cook something for them, so Erbil suggests getting them a takeaway from the local Bangladeshi restaurant. Erbil's gesture is such a relief to Janis and the two men are happy, discussing menus. The food smells great, but although he is hungry, Erbil decides to leave the three of them to enjoy the meal alone.

☆ ☆ ☆

Just before the party, Erbil makes his second visit to Janis's home. He is bringing her to see Amy in hospital before he takes her to the party at *Les Ambassadeurs* that evening. I have decided that Amy should know about her father's surprise birthday party, even if she can't attend. It is important, I feel, and Erbil is going to go with Janis to tell Amy that she is invited. He arrives to pick Janis up in a chauffeur-driven Jaguar, and finds her standing on the porch of her small house, a dress hanging from the door knob.

Janis has deliberated over what to wear to the party. She wants to look as good as Jane, who will also be present. The green dress she has chosen shows off her ankles and is very sexy, she confides to me. I have already told her that she should come to my hotel, where she can have her hair and make-up done in my suite.

After my first discussion with Janis, I initially believed that she had rethought her attitude towards Amy. After stating that there was nothing she could do about her daughter's problems, she called me to say that our conversation (which had covered everything from how Janis felt about herself and her relationship with her boyfriend to how she felt towards her daughter's problems) had been one of the best days in her life for a while and that it had 'been a wake-up call', which I took to mean about Amy.

I quickly realized, however, that what Janis meant was that it was a wake-up call about *her own life* and relationships. Before the party, Janis tells me that she is almost 90 percent sure that she will dump the boyfriend, who has hurt her feelings by refusing to sleep over at her house. On the other hand, she says, even though she is going to end the relationship, it would be great to be able to go to the party with him when she is looking so beautiful. Janis goes back and forth weighing up whether she should

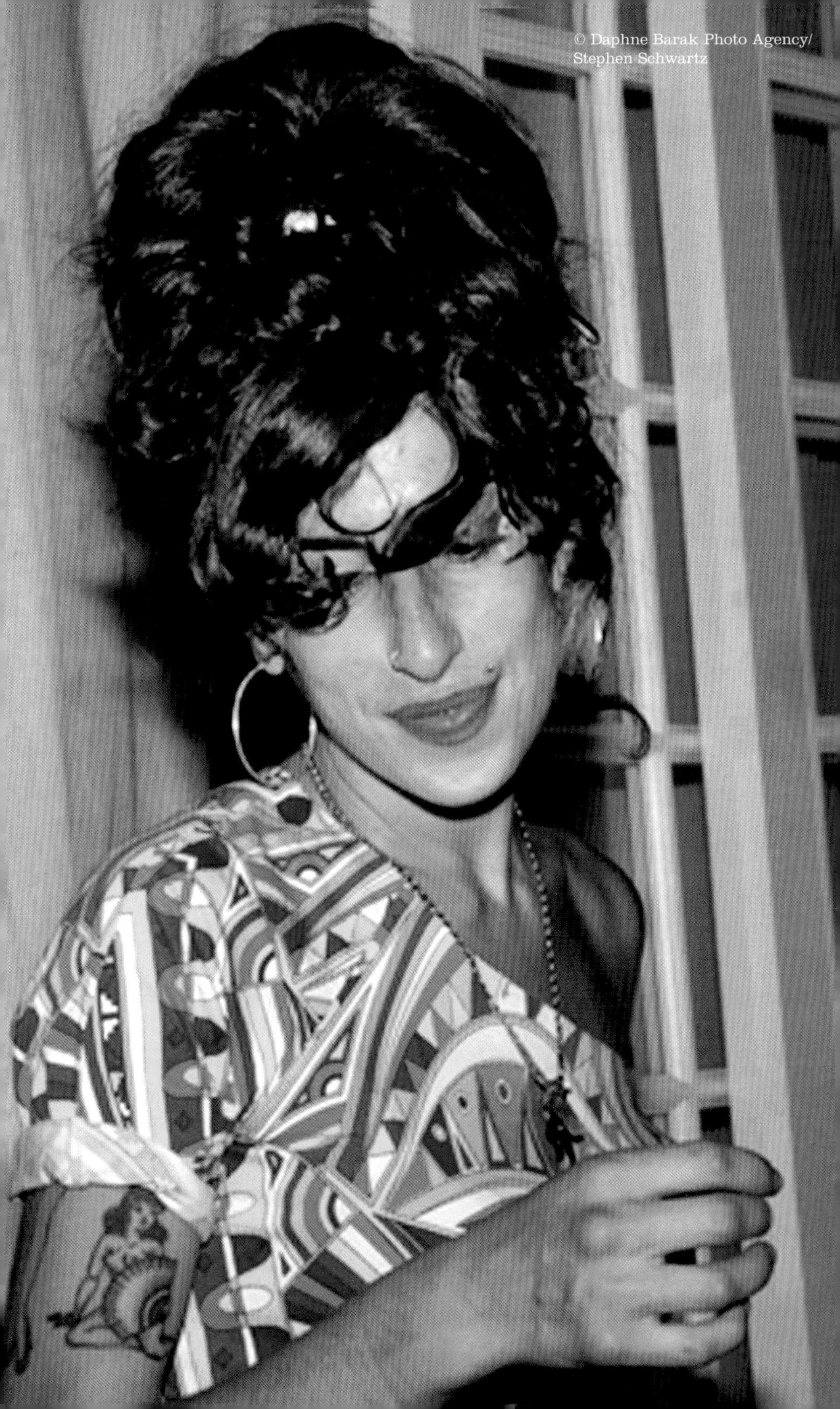

Above: Daphne, with Janis and Mitch in December 2008, at Les Ambassadeurs club, London.
Opposite: Amy in St. Lucia, April 2009.

Below: 'We did the best that we could in our own limited way… Maybe we could have done better, I don't know.' – Mitch Winehouse on raising Amy.

Above and below: Daphne with Mitch on Daphne's last night in St Lucia, April 2009.

Right: Amy in St Lucia, where she was meant to be recording her next album.

Below: Daphne with Amy in St Lucia, April 2009

© Daphne Barak Photo Agency/Erbil Gunasti

© Daphne Barak Photo Agency/Erbil Gunasti

© Daphne Barak Photo Agency/Erbil Gunasti

Opposite and above: In Amy's studio in St Lucia, April 2009. '... [A]ny song that she writes is like cutting an arm off. Every song is like pulling her heart out' – Mitch on Amy's songwriting process.

Above: Amy hugs her mother Janis in February 2008 after winning 5 out of 6 nominations, including Record of the Year for 'Rehab' at the Grammy Awards. She had to perform at the ceremony via satellite link as she was denied a Visa for the United States.

bring him or not. I finally tell her that it doesn't matter to me – that she just needs to decide what is best for her. When Erbil arrives to pick Janis up, the boyfriend is nowhere to be seen. Janis tells me later that they have split up.

On the hour-long drive to the hospital Janis talks to Erbil, pointing out various landmarks and places of interest, much as Mitch did when he took us around the East End and to Richmond. Erbil gets the strong feeling that Janis doesn't know what to expect from Amy when she sees her. She looks nervous and talks constantly about Amy. When approaching the hospital, Janis appears even more tense. When they arrive at the hospital, the chauffeur and Erbil both help Janis out of the car and Erbil walks slowly with her to the main entrance. It's not a big hospital by any means. With Erbil at her side, Janis walks towards reception, where she announces, 'We are here to see Amy Winehouse. I am her mother.'

Suddenly everyone becomes attentive and the people near the reception desk are all ears. They are quickly directed to the lift to take them to Amy's room, much to Erbil's surprise, as no one has asked for any proof of ID from either of them and Janis isn't a regular visitor to the hospital. Mitch told us that he left instructions that nobody should be permitted to go up to see Amy without him being alerted. Maybe the word 'mother' has magical powers!

Upstairs, they are directed towards the nurses' station, which is situated near the lift. There Janis is greeted by a few people, who obviously know who she is. They are Amy's security guards and one of them, Beatrice, tells Janis that Amy has been sleeping for a long time.

'Now that you are here you can wake her up,' she says to Janis. 'Only you can wake her … We can't do that, but you can.' She points to Amy's room, which is down the hallway. Then they disappear, leaving Janis and Erbil alone in the hallway.

Janis is obviously anxious and as they approach the door to Amy's room it seems to slam shut. Janis is holding onto Erbil's arm as they approach and he says reassuringly to her: 'Go ahead. Open the door and go in. … Wake her up.'

Janis opens the door a little but then stops, hesitating before asking him if he is coming in with her. Erbil tries to reassure this woman, this mother who seems frightened to enter her own daughter's room: 'Go in. I'll stay outside. Don't worry. That's the right thing to do. She has to wake up first … Let her take her time and wake her up slowly. Just sit there until she wakes up.' Janis looks at him unsure.

Erbil waits outside, feeling quite alone, but aware that Janis is probably feeling much more lonely behind the door. About 10 minutes pass before Janis opens the door to report to Erbil that she is OK and tell him that Amy is waking up. Erbil tells her to take it easy and let Amy wake up slowly. He tells her to close the door, which Janis does.

As he stands there, in the hallway, something odd happens. A couple with a little kid suddenly appear in the hallway, obviously walking towards Amy's room. Amy's guards are nowhere to be seen and Erbil is quite perplexed by these people, probably fans, who seem to think it's OK to knock on Amy's door. Before he can intervene, an unsuspecting Janis opens the door to be confronted by these strangers. She immediately calls Amy over to come and say 'Hi', much to Erbil's surprise. Seconds later, Amy, who looks like someone who has just woken from a deep sleep, and is dressed in short shorts and a T-shirt, appears from the darkness. Erbil thinks if he were in Amy's position he would probably behave badly; she's woken up to find not only Janis there but other strange people as well, including Erbil. But Amy smiles as she speaks to these loud-mouthed people who she doesn't know from Adam.

This is the first time that Erbil has met Amy in person and she is the consummate professional, very down-to-earth and very respectful of these people. When they leave, Erbil stays where he is and the door closes again. Minutes later, Amy appears again, this time dressed in a red jacket, clutching a couple of cigarettes. She walks past him to the end of the hallway where she disappears. Through the half-open door, Erbil can see Janis, sitting in the room; she looks worried. She tells Erbil that Amy hasn't said anything to her and obviously doesn't want to spend time with her as she has walked out of the room, leaving her mother behind.

Erbil says, 'She's the patient ... And she's not going anywhere. Just getting ... some air. Don't worry! She will be back soon. Just sit down and relax. You are her mother. You are here to invite her to the event. Show her the dress you plan to wear and ask her opinion.... See if she wants to join us. And then we'll go. In the meantime, just be patient. Let her be herself. She has just woken up from a long, deep sleep.'

Janis calms down and Erbil now has the time to take in the room. It is depressing, like most hospital rooms, and is small. Although it is obviously a private room, it hasn't got any windows. It is like a box and Erbil wonders how long Amy will agree to stay there.

Now Amy has left her room, Beatrice reappears, obviously pleased that her dirty work of waking up Amy has been done by someone else. Erbil is puzzled, however, as Beatrice brings in about half a dozen medium-sized shopping bags, containing food and bottles of drink, which she places next to the bathroom door. Amy doesn't eat that much, so who is all this for? And what else do the bags contain?

Amy doesn't seem to be that protected if anyone, family or strangers, can arrive unannounced and get into her room. Janis wasn't expected and Erbil could be anyone – a drug dealer even – as far as anyone knows. Amy is meant to be under surveillance 24–7 from what we all understand.

Suddenly Amy reappears, passing the nursing station, where she stops to talk to them briefly. She sees Erbil and gives him a polite but warm smile, as she speeds towards her waiting mother. Minutes later, Janis leaves the room, her expression blank. Erbil thinks that Janis must have told Amy about the party and asks her what her daughter's response is. Much to his surprise, Janis says that they haven't really discussed anything. Erbil asks Janis outright if she's invited Amy to the party and had a mother-daughter talk. Janis looks so dejected that Erbil leads her back to Amy's door. This time, he tells Janis to go in and tell Amy exactly why they are here and to show her the dress.

'Just spend some time with your daughter', he tells Janis. She cannot leave now. Erbil assures her that Amy will be happy to hear about the party and to see her choice of dress. She will want to hear all the details of the evening and share in her mother's excitement.

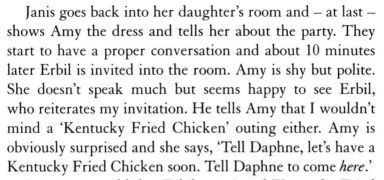

Janis goes back into her daughter's room and – at last – shows Amy the dress and tells her about the party. They start to have a proper conversation and about 10 minutes later Erbil is invited into the room. Amy is shy but polite. She doesn't speak much but seems happy to see Erbil, who reiterates my invitation. He tells Amy that I wouldn't mind a 'Kentucky Fried Chicken' outing either. Amy is obviously surprised and she says, 'Tell Daphne, let's have a Kentucky Fried Chicken soon. Tell Daphne to come *here*.'

It may seem odd that Erbil mentioned 'Kentucky Fried Chicken' during his first conversation with Amy, but he knew what he was doing when he said it. Erbil was referring to something that Mitch had already told us. When Mitch comes to see her, Amy always says, 'Daddy. Let's go have a KFC!' or 'Daddy, bring some KFC!' And this is her way of breaking the ice between them, so Erbil turns this round on her.

Erbil replies, 'Daphne would love to have a Kentucky Fried Chicken with you! I promise to introduce you to Daphne!' Amy gives him a cheerful smile and agrees.

☆ ☆ ☆

There is one thing that strikes me quite strongly about Janis's visit to the hospital. Here is Amy's mother, visiting her sick, only daughter, something that she isn't able to do every day – and she hasn't brought her anything. I am not talking about bringing a gift for a stranger, but a present for her own daughter, something that she knows Amy might be missing – some food that she's cooked for her or a special cream that Amy uses. Similarly, if Amy is suddenly able to come to the party, what will she wear? Janis hasn't brought her a dress or heels. Amy has these white heels, so high you would need to be an acrobat to walk in them, and even I know they are her favourite shoes, but Janis hasn't brought them with her.

I have absolutely no doubt that Janis loves Amy, but it doesn't occur to her to do these things for her daughter. Perhaps because Janis is so alone and so grateful for any attention given to her, something she makes clear when we pay her compliments or make her feel special in any way, she fails to see that Amy also craves that same attention and love. Or perhaps she is just scared of being rejected by her daughter.

☆ ☆ ☆

Supported by Erbil, Janis leaves the hospital happy. She has achieved her mission and has delivered the invitation to the party to Amy and when she leaves her daughter, Amy is smiling. Janis comes to my hotel nearby, where she goes through hair and make-up in my suite. When she shows up at the party, everybody is buzzing about her appearance. *'Look how beautiful Janis is!'*

Janis talks to Amy's assistant, Chivan, and then to a bodyguard. *Now*, she has the courage to ask them to make sure that Amy 'really knows she is invited – and welcome'. I leave Janis with my team, and a new confidence.

Amy's mother, who looks so much like Amy, clings onto me while an impatient Mitch makes a speech to family and friends about filming *Saving Amy*. His pretty wife, Jane, is hugging him as he explains about the documentary. He flatters me, telling the audience how I have interviewed Nelson Mandela and Prince Charles and played host to Hillary Clinton in my home. He thanks Erbil, Bitu and also my brother, who helped design a website for Mitch. He says, *'Our family has been facing this very painful experience …'*.

At that moment I push Janis forward towards Mitch, saying to her *'It is your daughter'*. I say this in a very friendly manner as she is an essential part of this as well, but Mitch doesn't have the brains to include her. Janis takes the microphone and speaks from the heart just as Mitch does. It is an extremely moving scene – a family pulling together for their child – and everyone is applauding because Mitch, Janis, his ex-wife, and Jane, his second wife, hug each other, united as they pray for Amy's recovery and for other families to avoid what they are going through. Only Amy is missing.

Mitch carries on speaking, this time about his wife and ex-wife who stand next to him: *'Okay these women are just fantastic. They are strong women, Janis and Jane. I love them both. Only Jane just a little bit more…'*

It is an awkward moment and everyone looks uncomfortable. Poor Jane is standing there all lovely and smiling, trying to support her man and be nice to Janis, but while Mitch and Janis talk, she says nothing. She quite often says nothing.

Then Mitch starts singing Sinatra. He has a good, powerful and full voice. It is very clear where Amy gets her voice and passion for music from. He is entertaining and it's no surprise that he has a record deal now.

While Mitch is singing songs including 'Strangers in the Night' and 'New York, New York' and his family and

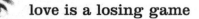

friends are dancing, Erbil is busy talking to Amy's people at the hospital. On the one hand, it is clear that Mitch doesn't really want his daughter to be at the party and embarrass him on his Big Day. On the other hand, and I feel Janis and the others agree with me, it is only fair that Amy is invited, and is not made to feel a lesser being because of her addictions. If she feels up to coming, she should do so. So, while I am hosting Mitch, Janis, Alex and his lovely girlfriend, and family and friends, Erbil and Amy's people are debating whether she should attend.

The final decision is that she is not well enough. I think, *'Let it be. This is what Mitch wants, anyhow …'*

I ask Jane and Melody, Mitch's sister, to serve him the huge birthday cake that has been prepared. I call out to him, *'Mitch, make a wish!'*

Before blowing the candle, a tearful Mitch says: *'Well, everyone here knows what my only one wish is …'* Of course, he is talking about Amy getting better.

A few minutes later when we are having photos taken and are being entertained by Mitch's musician friends, I spot him sitting by himself. He is a very lonely figure.

As I join him, I ask him if everything is OK.

When he sees me, he tries to perk up, saying, 'Oh Daphne! Great party. My family and friends love it. I am *so* grateful.'

Then he adds quietly, '… But I *miss* my daughter. *I wish she could be here.'*

amy, amy, amy

The morning after the party, Mitch and Jane, who have slept over at my hotel as usual, are having coffee with us. Mitch tells me that the doctors have called him as Amy wants to leave the hospital! Of course, Mitch needs to blame someone and he says, *'It's because Erbil and Janis visited Amy'*. I had told him about their visit earlier in the evening, when I explained to him that we had invited Amy but she wasn't well enough to attend the party.

Mitch says 'Daphne if *she* came to the party, it would be embarrassing for me.' I look at him disapprovingly, so he quickly adds, 'And – she [wouldn't] have anything to wear.' I am slightly confused by Mitch's attitude. Hasn't he just gathered his family and close friends to tell them all about our *Saving Amy* project? And he also talks of how he wants to help, 'at least one family …'. Mitch doesn't mind discussing Amy's problems publicly but even amongst his own family, he is apparently now 'embarrassed' by her?

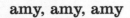

Jane also surprises me by having strong opinions about Amy attending. I feel sorry for Janis, as she is Amy's mother and it isn't really Jane's business. But Jane has had a tough few weeks, having to deal with being made redundant, although she has now found a new job. While Mitch is at the hospital much of the time with his daughter, Jane has had to cope with the loss of her job largely by herself.

During that time, when Mitch says, 'I have to go to Amy's hospital', I hear Jane exclaim on at least five or six occasions, 'Oh, no!'

This is not because Jane dislikes Amy, but rather that she isn't always able to deal with the constant battle for Mitch's attention, not just with Amy but with Janis as well. She wants a normal family life with Mitch.

Amy's trip to St Lucia in December is born of this dilemma. Amy doesn't want to stay in hospital anymore and has confronted the doctors about discharging herself. They can't force Amy to stay in the hospital because she isn't sick – at least, not physically.

There is also the question of where she will go. Janis is scheduled to go to Miami for medical treatment for her MS and Mitch and Jane are meant to be going to the Canary Islands for a much-needed break. Mitch has also been looking for a new house for his daughter. He and Janis don't want Amy to go back to her old home, just in case Blake is released from prison and goes back there – but that house isn't ready yet.

I look at Mitch and voice what I think is a natural solution to their problem, that he and Jane postpone their trip until January, after Amy is installed in her new home.

'What is the big deal?' I say. 'It is not as if you have a 9 to 5 job, right? Your job is to save Amy.'

Mitch immediately pipes up, 'No. No. I can't. Jane will divorce me. We have already promised friends. We *have* to go.'

At that point it isn't even about Jane's schedule at work because she is about to be made redundant. It's about Jane – and Mitch's promise to her that they will go.

'Jane will divorce me. I promised Jane,' he repeats.

Their marriage has a lot of problems and it is very easy to lay them all at Amy's door, but Mitch is essentially torn between at least two women on a day-to-day basis – his second wife and Amy (three, if one includes Janis).

Mitch had told me earlier that Amy has, on occasion, treated Jane badly in the past. He recounts one incident when Amy went to his home and stole Jane's perfume. I comment that everyone knows that stealing or lying is common among addicts.

However, Mitch carries on, saying that when he confronted Amy about the incident, she didn't really understand what the issue was and her response was to send Jane an expensive gift instead.

He explains, 'It is not about that. It is about the fact that Jane didn't want an expensive gift. She wanted her *own* perfume.'

That is probably true, but given the context – that one person is a mature woman, who knows she is dealing with someone with problems, and the other is an addict, who lies and steals, and doesn't necessarily think rationally – it seems a bit ridiculous for Mitch to torment himself over whose side he should take. It is so much wasted energy for

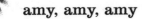

him. But perhaps he, albeit unknowingly, enjoys being in the midst of the three demanding women in his life.

I understand it is difficult for Jane. She rarely speaks in Mitch's presence. Maybe she used to want to say more but now, perhaps, I think she chooses not to. The only time I really hear her express what she wants is when she and Mitch visit my vacation home, which I've already spoken about (*see page 101*).

While there, it is obvious that Mitch needs to unload, which I understand, but it goes on for hours and hours, with poor Jane just listening. Mitch means so well, but when Jane breaks in and says she wants to be part of it all, that she wants to help, his response is to try to cuddle her and say, '*Well, yes of course*'. But Jane just repeats, '*I want to be involved*'.

It is a very tense moment and shows that while Mitch has huge problems with Amy, he also has them with Jane, who needs more attention from him and wants to be more involved in decision-making.

Mitch, however, is a control freak and needs to at least think he is calling all the shots. Even though I am very sympathetic about what he is going through with Amy, in a way, it is transparent that he uses Amy as an excuse. It is very convenient for him to say to Jane, 'You have listened to me for years and you are so patient, but I can give you *this* amount of attention as I have such a sick daughter to deal with.'

And that is why their marriage has problems – not because of Amy but because of Mitch's excuses and his battle to please, as he sees it, Amy, Jane and, even to a certain extent, Janis, as well.

So ... Amy is sent to St Lucia because Mitch thinks Jane will divorce him if he postpones their holiday plans, although Mitch tries to convince me that it's his daughter's decision.

'Amy wants to go to St Lucia,' Mitch says to me as we are having dinner the night before she is due to fly out to the Caribbean island. But Mitch is tense: his face is so red that it makes me concerned about his health. He is scared that his daughter won't make the flight and that the family's vacation plans will be affected.

The following day, he calls me, just to assure me that everything is OK.

'She made the flight,' he says.

Amy's friends slept over to make sure that she got on the plane. Mitch is obviously relieved. But, all I can think is, you have to question how on earth an addict dealing with alcohol problems ends up vacationing in a resort with free booze.

☆ ☆ ☆

In late December, photographs of Amy, without her trademark beehive and sporting short curly hair instead, frolicking topless in the waves in St Lucia or relaxing with friends, are published in the media. Reports also emerge that while Amy looks healthier and more curvaceous than she has done in recent months, she is out drinking heavily in bars on the island.

Then in January, while I am hosting a surprise birthday party for my producer at a London restaurant at which Mitch is present, we receive a call telling us that Amy has

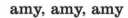

been spilling her guts to no less than a reporter from the British Sunday paper *News of the World*.

She has reportedly been talking about sex, drugs, and more sex ... Blake is going mad, having heard about Amy's alleged affair with a younger man while she's been away and is reportedly seeking a divorce and half of Amy's fortune. Mitch looks like someone has shot him. He leaves the birthday party shortly after the call. I am surprised as Mitch should be happy with the news of the divorce: after all this is what he and Janis have wanted for such a long time.

There is one problem, however – Amy.

Mitch shows up at my hotel two days after the party and confirms that the divorce proceedings are, indeed, official: 'My solicitors were served the papers by Blake's solicitors. However ... I don't know what to do. ... Amy doesn't understand why he wants to divorce her? I had to call her before she heard about it from someone else. ... She asked me "Daddy, why does he want to divorce me?" I had to say: "Listen, you know I don't like him. *I hate him.* But I have to admit that your behaviour with another man is not really what marriage is all about."'

Mitch flies out to St Lucia to be with his daughter. He asks me to join them but the flights and the emotions are too complicated – so I bail out. While he is on the plane Amy is photographed on all fours, prowling for alcohol, after bar staff refused to serve her. She has also allegedly been begging holidaymakers to get alcohol for her.

The papers openly question why Amy, who is fighting addictions to both drink and drugs, has been sent to the Le Sport Spa for a 'health kick'.

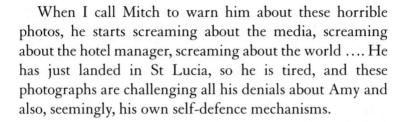

When I call Mitch to warn him about these horrible photos, he starts screaming about the media, screaming about the hotel manager, screaming about the world …. He has just landed in St Lucia, so he is tired, and these photographs are challenging all his denials about Amy and also, seemingly, his own self-defence mechanisms.

☆ ☆ ☆

I am trying to rearrange my schedule to visit Amy in St Lucia. In the meantime, Janis manages to visit her daughter. Mitch has already visited Amy twice by this stage, but it is much more difficult for Janis to travel, given her medical condition.

Janis and another female relative visit Amy for some quiet time. It is meant to be a surprise, Janis tells me. And at that time, most people are speculating about when Amy will return to England to talk to Blake about the proposed divorce.

Janis tells me that when Amy is informed that she has arrived in St Lucia and is staying next door, she screams, *'Mummy, Mummy, Mummy.'*

Amy is delighted to see them. It brings back happy childhood memories, apparently, but after a brief reunion she leaves the two women and heads to the gym.

Her mother tells me: 'She has changed so much since I saw her last in London. She looks wonderful. She is different … Like someone who has got a new life – *different.*'

Janis enjoyed her vacation in St Lucia. She recalls, 'We had this apartment on the beach. It was next door to

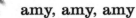

Amy so we could have … easy access without the media following up.'

However, the mother and daughter bonding time ends up being very brief. Janis tells me that from the first day of their visit, Amy's tied up trying to get an early flight back to London, but with little success.

She describes one of her memorable encounters with her daughter, one that took place in late February 2009. The two women are sitting having lunch on the beach. They are being treated like VIPs and that is obviously because of Amy.

'We were relaxed,' she says. 'Besides catching up with Amy, we needed to catch up with each other.'

'We didn't mind [that] we hardly saw Amy because I am her mother! I know how much she loves me. I never demand. And then, Amy showed up with her friend, Violet. She came and kissed me goodbye. She was leaving to … go back to London. She [had] found a flight via Barbados. Then she continued to say goodbye to other people. She disappeared from my sight. Then … reappeared …'

Janis recalls that it was like a scene from a movie.

'… My Amy was riding on a black horse! She was bowing towards me. … This horse's name was "Black Beauty"!

'I learnt that Amy coordinated it with a person who is in charge of the horses there. But it was such a magical moment.

'[We] were just looking [on] in disbelief. Then she jumped off the horse, came and kissed us and faded away. … Can you imagine what a life I have?!'

☆ ☆ ☆

Amy flew back into Gatwick Airport near London on 1 March 2009. On the 2nd, *People* magazine reported that Amy was sporting her old beehive hairstyle and hanging out with Mitch in her new North London home. Blake had been released from prison again and sources revealed that Amy was determined to persuade her husband not to divorce her; while other sources close to Blake revealed that he was determined to make the break.

Just days later, Amy was back in the press again, this time charged with assault over allegedly hitting a fan in September of the previous year. She was due to appear in court to face charges on 17 March, which she did, appearing late, to plead not guilty. The case was then adjourned until July 2009.

Later in March, Amy confirmed that she would be performing in the Island Records 50th anniversary celebrations to be held in May, along with such artists as Paul Weller, Sly & Robbie and Keane. But by April, Amy was back in St Lucia again, this time to record her third album, again with Salaam Remi, who had worked with her on both of her earlier albums. It was announced that Amy would also perform at the St Lucia Jazz Festival in May and then fly back to England to perform in the Island Record celebrations.

☆ ☆ ☆

I was with Mitch in a Moroccan restaurant on 3 April 2009 when he told me that Amy was leaving for St Lucia to work on her album and that he would also be joining her on the 23rd. Mitch needed to see me. He felt that I was neglecting him because of my other commitments.

'This time you are coming, right Daphne?'

I have already had to cancel visiting Amy in St Lucia, due to other commitments and the 23rd in terms of my work schedule seems a long way off, but I tell Mitch that I will try, even though it is also my birthday about that time.

He says, 'This time I am flying First Class. ... I don't care because Universal is paying for my ticket. The record company is paying for ... my ticket, for her ticket and the villa accommodation because she is going to ... work on a record ....'

I say 'OK,' but I am puzzled. As we leave the restaurant, I think: 'Wow! He doesn't really get it. The record company isn't paying for his lavish villa and First Class travel. They are taking some of Amy's income and giving it to him....' And, as long as she produces another record, who cares?

A few days before we fly to St Lucia – even though I have requested a suite for me, Erbil and Steve Schwartz, my stills photographer – Mitch's travel agent calls to say that she is taking a villa for us, one of four sited together: one for Amy; one for Mitch and his friends; one for the recording studio and the technicians; and we will have the fourth.

Mitch informs me that Amy is going to play at the St Lucia Jazz Festival. When I ask him who else is playing, he reels off a few familiar names, such as KC and the Sunshine Band and a few other 'Golden Oldies', making it sound as if Amy is just one among many musicians and it's not a big deal. Three weeks later, when we are in

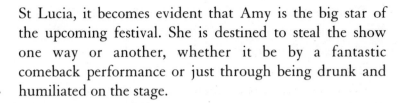

St Lucia, it becomes evident that Amy is the big star of the upcoming festival. She is destined to steal the show one way or another, whether it be by a fantastic comeback performance or just through being drunk and humiliated on the stage.

☆ ☆ ☆

In the end we are able to go to St Lucia in April. We arrive on Friday 24th, a day later than everyone else as they have come from London. Erbil and I have come from Paris and Steve has come from New York.

The four villas are in Cotton Bay Village and are situated literally a minute from the beach. Our villa is next door to Amy's and beyond that is the converted record studio, where Amy is rehearsing for the festival and recording; the last one is for Mitch and his friends. Two executives from Universal Studios have also joined us for two days. The whole place is very relaxing and very beautiful. It is also very private, and the place is patrolled – day and night – by a security team. Mitch tells me that Amy is very happy here.

But when I land, I find a worried text message from Mitch, telling me how difficult it is for him to cope: '*She [Amy] is drinking a lot ... I can't take it.*'

I feel for him, especially while I am on the helicopter to the hotel – the friendly pilot is making some funny reference to Amy's well-documented wild behaviour on the island. Erbil and I both stare at my Blackberry quietly. I just pray that the pilot hasn't shared his brand of humour with Mitch or his friends.

When we arrive at the hotel, the manager, Kevin, is there to receive us in person – he apologizes as my villa will not be ready for a couple of hours and he leads us to the bar area on the beach.

We spot Amy immediately – sitting at the bar, drinking and chatting loudly, even at this early hour of the morning. It is actually sad to watch, so we keep our distance and she leaves after a little while.

We later meet up with Mitch, who is wearing shorts and flip-flops. He is so happy to see us! I immediately give him a supportive hug, and tell him – referring to his text message from a few hours before – that I understand it must be very painful for him to watch his daughter ruining herself. But, to our amazement, Mitch tell us, 'No, no. She is doing fantastic. No, she only drank one or two glasses …'.

Instead, we start chatting happily about our plans for the day. Mitch says to me, 'Amy knows you're coming. You will meet her soon.' When I mention briefly that we have, in fact, already seen her, he turns to the corner of the bar, where she was drinking just half an hour ago and asks me, 'Oh! She was THERE? Was she drinking?!' I avoid his eyes and his question, and quickly change the topic of conversation.

Later, while we are relaxing by the pool in Mitch's villa, Amy dashes in, dressed in her trademark bikini top and tight shorts, which show off the fact that one of her legs is badly bruised. After a little hesitation, Amy jumps on me, clinging to me and showering me with kisses. Then she kisses Erbil and gestures that she remembers he promised to introduce me! He kisses her back.

Amy is now excited about our arrival and decides that she wants to throw us a welcome dinner that evening. She counts out how many people it will be for, discusses the menu lovingly with us and then tells me, 'You don't have to dress up.'

Amy keeps coming back to see us again and again that afternoon, making plans for the evening. Meanwhile Mitch, Erbil and I are at the swimming pool with another couple, Paul and Beverly. Mitch and Paul are playing water games and we are all laughing, enjoying ourselves. It seems that apart from work, this trip will be a normal, relaxing vacation.

Later that evening Mitch leads us across the sand towards a bonfire on the beach that has been built specially to help us get to the place where we are dining. When we arrive, Amy – dressed in a mini-mini orange dress – is already there, waiting rather anxiously for us.

She hugs me, introducing us all to her close friend, Vicky (Victoria), who appears to be a lovely woman; she lives on St Lucia with her partner. Vicky explains that she almost didn't come to the dinner as there had been a big accident, just days before our arrival, which had made the St Lucia headlines, and she had had to attend two funerals that day. But, Amy had requested that she come tonight: 'I couldn't say "No"', she says.

Amy whispers in a very childish manner, 'That is when you know somebody is your friend, Daphne. She is my close friend.' Vicky and her partner had met Amy two weeks earlier at the resort.

Mitch overhears Amy's comment, and gives me a pained, anxious look.

We are joined by some more of Amy's new friends: an Italian woman, her husband, brother-in-law, their young seven- or eight-year-old daughter and her friend, who is the daughter of the British High Commissioner. It is the last two guests that cause Amy the most excitement. She leaves the table, spending a lot of time with them, choreographing dance routines for them and playing with them. Amy may be 25 but she is so petite that she can almost be mistaken for one of the girls.

Even though it is clear that she is far more happy and much more secure in the girls' company than with us adults, she is going out of her way to please me. She places napkins across my lap, slowly, one at a time, covering my dress completely.

Although everyone is staring at us, because Amy keeps saying, 'Daphne I want to take good care of you', I try to keep things casual.

There is a lot of food, which she insists on serving us, insisting too that everyone should start with rice on their plates. Amy is obviously shaking as she dishes out the food. She can hardly hold the plates. At one point, as she struggles to cut a piece of fish, she just sinks her fingers into the flesh, grabbing whatever she can. But she is fundamentally playing with her food. Most people don't seem to realize this, as she makes a big fuss of feeding us, but she is just moving her food around her plate. Has she really overcome her bulimia and anorexia?

Later I give Amy a gift. It's just something fun – a set of lip gloss, made by my friend Melina Belafonte. Amy is shaking and struggles to open the little box; she soon loses patience when she can't figure out how to open it. I end up opening it for her, after which she asks her security people to bring her a make-up pencil, which she applies to her mouth with a trembling hand. The now-open lip-gloss box seems to make her nervous for some reason. Only when I tell her that it is a beauty line made by Melina, the wife of David, Harry Belafonte's son, does she start screaming, 'Oh! … Daphne knows Harry Belafonte!'

During the evening Amy disappears often to smoke and, as her worried father, Mitch, suspects … to drink. But her insecurity and her tremendous efforts to please, as well as her constant need to hug everyone around her, make you just want to hug her back and tell her that everything will be all right.

At some point during the long dinner, Amy disappears. When we walk back to my villa after the dinner, she reappears, her security man in tow, as she heads to her villa, which is next door to mine. She has changed her dress for another skimpy blue number. She looks at me, hesitantly. She does not know what to do. The grown-up world is so complicated for her.

I say, 'Thank you, sweetie, for dinner. It was lovely.' And she just looks *so* relieved.

Amy hugs me and then goes to hug Erbil too, saying, 'I am so glad you enjoyed it. It was so important to me.'

☆ ☆ ☆

'It is private here,' Mitch comments later. 'Even though the place is full you never see anybody. It's great.'

'So, it is relaxing?' I ask him.

'Yeah,' he agrees. 'Very relaxing. … Very secure, very

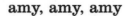

private … You can hear the music now,' he says, meaning the drumming coming from the recording studio villa.

'[The] equipment has been brought over from London and from Miami,' Mitch says. 'All the equipment is in there – as if it were a normal studio. It is a very, very nice vibe in there.'

'… She is getting ready for the jazz festival and also she is preparing her new album,' he explains, 'but this is where she is relaxed. This is where she feels good. This is where it is all happening. She is very happy here.'

'Protected?' I say.

'Very protected.'

I suggest that he shows me round the studio.

He leads me in. There is a huge amount of equipment lying around, which Mitch says is just spare. We go through the kitchen and come across Amy sitting at the drums.

'Hello, Dad, I have got a song for you. Watch me play the drums to this. You will like this,' she comments, as she kisses Mitch, adding, 'I am not as good as you!'

'Hello Daphne!' she embraces me, kissing me hello, before going back to play the drums.

'She is just jamming at the moment,' Mitch comments, watching his daughter.

'Do you think she should stick to singing?' he adds, after a moment.

'Let's have a go Amy. Something jazzy,' he says.

Amy moves away and he takes his daughter's place. He starts to play the drums.

'Well?' he asks me, after a few seconds.

'You are good,' I acknowledge.

'No!' he denies, still drumming.

'My Dad is really good,' Amy confirms. 'Honestly.'

'He is. He is,' I repeat, as I watch Amy watch her father perform.

Mitch is so emotional that he takes me dancing to celebrate my birthday.

☆ ☆ ☆

I meet Amy, who is dressed in a gold bikini top, at the bar next to the beach. She says she is planning a celebration for me for my birthday. I ask her, teasingly, whether she is going to perform 'Happy Birthday' to me, à la Marilyn Monroe's legendary singing to President John F. Kennedy. Amy says that she would like to, but she doesn't have the right outfit with her!

She orders some food but then disappears, only to return with a three-year-old boy called Ricky trailing after her. Amy feeds him, instead of feeding herself. When he drops his lollipop, she rushes out to wash it for him. Ricky's parents don't seem to be around and Amy has seemingly taken over the role of mother of the boy. I am reminded of Mitch's comment that Amy always wants to help others more than she wants to help herself.

Even with this responsibility, she manages to disappear every few minutes, asking Mitch to watch Ricky when she does. Later someone spots her at her usual section of the bar, gulping down a drink.

When she comes back, she peers at the green-coloured cocktail I am drinking and asks what's in it.

'You wouldn't like it – it's not sweet,' I tell her.

She tries it anyway, but makes a face. Then asks, 'Does

it have alcohol?'

When I admit that it does, she raises the glass again to her lips. Within seconds she has drained two-thirds of my drink. Mitch and I exchange glances. Has she swapped one addiction for another? Is she doing it to punish him? Herself? Why?

Then Amy starts to chat with me about her piercings. She tells me that the one on her mouth is not painful and can be removed. She opens her mouth wide to show Mitch and I both sides of the piercing. Then she shows us the piercing on her nose.

'This one I did it myself ...'. She sees my expression, and adds, 'No it wasn't that painful ...'

Then she tells us that she didn't have a problem removing the piercing from her nipple. 'But the one I have here' – she points to her vagina – 'is harder to remove. But one day when I had sex with Blake – when we finished – I looked at the cushion and found the piercing lying there ... It just got out.'

She continues to talk about Blake, who is currently suing for divorce and is also alleged to have got another woman pregnant. From the way she discusses him, in a dry, detached tone, I don't get the impression that it is her one and only obsession to see him at that time. But my feeling is that she does not actually understand that a real divorce is happening back in England. On the other hand, Blake's name is obviously not taboo. Not even in Mitch's presence – Mitch, who has been pushing for the divorce – trying to save her.

☆ ☆ ☆

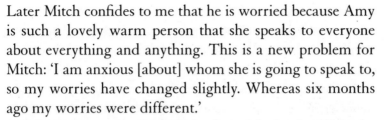

Later Mitch confides to me that he is worried because Amy is such a lovely warm person that she speaks to everyone about everything and anything. This is a new problem for Mitch: 'I am anxious [about] whom she is going to speak to, so my worries have changed slightly. Whereas six months ago my worries were different.'

'Six months ago you thought she might be dead?' I ask.

'I don't know about that – but she was certainly on the verge of being ill, so … the progress that she has made has been astonishing.'

'You say she speaks to everybody openly. She doesn't have the judgement, right? She is too open.'

'Perhaps,' Mitch says quietly.

☆ ☆ ☆

'It's still a very bumpy road …,' he says to me. 'There have been many relapses [since around Christmas]. She didn't [give up drugs] all of a sudden; she was talking about it for two or three months. Then she checked all the options and favoured going to substitute drugs.

'Look, there will be more relapses,' he continues. 'But who would believe, six months ago, that we'd be at this stage? That she'd be walking, laughing, hosting dinner for you, singing? It's amazing. My daughter seems happy.'

But is she happy, I wonder?

☆ ☆ ☆

On the island, over the next few days, Mitch seems to continually waver between telling everyone how much

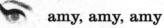

better Amy is doing – that she's wonderful, especially now she is finally about to start recording – and then becoming more and more edgy about the forthcoming jazz festival and Amy's condition.

He says, 'Why did I agree to this? Maybe she should never perform … just record. … It is like it used to be. But instead of drugs, it is alcohol. She will never be better.'

wake up
alone

On the night of my birthday, Amy hugs me as we make the short journey between our villas. She has pulled out all the stops, and has dressed up in high heels and a minuscule dress. So tiny that it has upset Mitch.

Amy holds onto me, complaining as we walk together: 'My Dad thinks it is too short.'

'But of course!' I say to her, 'All Dads are like that. They [do] not like their daughters to look ... inviting.'

And I add that she should take it as a compliment because she looks so sexy. Amy loves this and suddenly what she has previously perceived as a rejection by Mitch is turned into something more positive.

As I start greeting friends, I overhear Amy telling someone, *'Daphne said I am sexy. She said I am sexy!'*

We open a bottle of champagne to toast my birthday. While everybody is waiting to be served, Amy drinks one glass – bottoms up – in one rapid swallow. She then looks

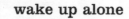

at me and, obviously recalling my tongue-in-cheek request of earlier that day, she starts to sing – imitating Monroe's famous 'Happy Birthday, Mr President …'.

For a few seconds, the shaky insecure Amy of moments earlier becomes so powerful, so strong. I am relieved that she still has such a fantastic voice and is such an obvious talent. We give her a standing ovation. Amy bows to me; then to her father and our friends.

Then she runs off to change the mini dress that her father has so disapproved of.

☆ ☆ ☆

We are going to dinner at a restaurant named Big Chef as Amy wants to celebrate my birthday there.

When we arrive – without Amy – we are offered menus, but Mitch seems very reluctant to order. He seems uncomfortable, on edge and anxious about whether Amy will turn up, or not. I say, of course she will. He is so exhausted at this point that I add: 'Let's order. Let's not wait for her.'

A bodyguard shows up, informing us that Amy is not coming. While Mitch's face begins to show his anger at this news, Amy, giggling, shows up – this time in an even shorter dress, which is red with a pink zipper at the back. She comes and sits next to me, acting like a naughty little girl. She hugs me as I point to her dress and say in wonder, 'Amy! … another Hervé Léger dress! I have many of his dresses and none of them is *that* short!'

Amy asks me to stand up and then – in the middle of the crowded restaurant – she starts undressing behind me, showing me how she has folded the Léger bandage dress from a knee length outfit to sit just below what would make you blush. I tell her that knee length would make her look much sexier but she ignores my suggestion, complaining instead that she doesn't have a new dress for her performance at the May jazz festival. 'I mean all the dresses I have here are not good. I have worn them already,' she says.

To appease her, I tell her not to worry: I have a couple of new Légers in my luggage and she can have one as a gift. They are very expensive, straight from Paris, and this seems to make Amy feel much better. But, as it turns out, this is only for a short while.

Less than half an hour later, Mitch is very upset once again. Amy has been rude to a guest – the female executive from Universal, it seems, who offered Amy food.

Our whole table is upside down as Mitch scowls at his daughter, who looks at him, upset, waiting for a sign of his obvious disapproval.

Amy finally walks away, looking like a little girl who is being punished by being sent to the corner. She comes over to me, hugging me as she starts to cry. 'I need to go right now,' she murmurs, in between tears. 'My Daddy wants me to go. *I have been a bad girl.* I drank too much …'

She is obviously extremely upset and leans against me as she weeps. I try to calm her down, commenting that all of us do many things 'too much' at one time or another, like eating and drinking, and the mature thing is to deal with it and move on.

As Mitch passes by, I almost force Amy to face him. 'Your father loves you very much!' I add, as I urge her

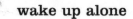

towards him. She is sobbing. Mitch still looks very angry. Even when we go outside to take my birthday photographs, he is reluctant to hug his daughter or do anything that might signal his approval. She hugs me instead – tightly.

She needs to be loved and approved of. But as Mitch says to me later that night: 'I *can't* approve [of] her addiction and drinking. She should know that.'

And frankly – he has a point.

☆ ☆ ☆

On the way out of the restaurant Amy, who has been clutching a deck of tarot cards the whole evening, stops me. She sits herself down at a table near the entrance and starts shuffling the cards.

Amy explains that her Nana Cynthia knew how to 'do it'.

'To read the future?' I query.

'Yes,' Amy says. 'Cynthia knew …'

'I heard about your grandma Cynthia and how close you were,' I comment.

'Yes,' Amy replies. 'I miss Cynthia.'

Both Mitch and Janis have spoken at length about Cynthia and her influence on their daughter. I recall Mitch saying that Amy's behaviour and attitude began to noticeably deteriorate after his mother's death in 2006.

☆ ☆ ☆

The next day, Mitch comes to my villa. He is obviously distressed and looks tired and fed up. 'Amy has been drinking from [early this] morning,' he says.

'I don't think I will come here, again,' he says wearily. '... She said to me today "Dad, thank you for pulling me out of drugs" and I said to her, "No, I didn't. ... I was there for you. I am your father. But you are the one who decided to pull out. You can do it again and stop drinking."'

I do feel for Mitch at that point! One can't really judge a father who looks so exhausted after battling his daughter's addictions.

'Look,' he tells me. 'I knew it will be a bumpy road. I knew there [would] be relapses. But after she almost died twice, to see her walking, smiling ... she has progressed so much.

'If you saw her in that dark room, in bed ... you couldn't believe we would be sitting here and she [would] be hosting [a] dinner for you. But now, if it is alcohol instead of hard drugs – I don't think I can go ... through the same thing [again]. I decided to distance myself – and whatever happens, happens. It is her life. It is her career. It is her decision.'

☆ ☆ ☆

By Monday, the tension between them is palpable. And Mitch is not just worried about Amy's behaviour and drinking but also about the effect of her 'new best friends' on his daughter.

I decide to reciprocate and pay back Amy's hospitality. I am going to throw a barbecue at my villa or Mitch's for everyone – Amy, her producer and engineers, the security detail, and Mitch and his close friends. They all love the idea, including Amy, it seems. The guys ask for lots of 'chicken wings' ... not KFC ...

Part of the reason for having a barbecue is that I have observed that Amy can't handle a sit-down meal, where people are watching and are looking at your plate. With a barbecue, it is more relaxed and people stand around and come when they want to. We decide to hold it at Mitch's villa since his swimming pool is bigger.

I bump into Andrew, Amy's bodyguard, in the bar, and discuss the barbecue with him. Amy is also there, already drinking even though it is still quite early. She is sitting with her new best friend Vicky and is already quite drunk. Amy's body language is quite hostile and she mumbles that she and her band are far too busy to attend the barbecue that just a little while ago had got her so excited. She probably will have to record all night, she says, although by her current behaviour, she's not really in a fit enough state to record anything. The musicians and bodyguards seem quite used to her sudden change in mood.

She deliberately turns her back on us. Her behaviour is becoming increasingly nasty. Then she begins to talk loudly about her parents to Vicky. She says dismissively, '*Forget* my father. You are the one I am going to consult about my clothes and about which music I should pick for my records, for the jazz festival.'

Vicky is delighted at this and seems to encourage Amy in her nasty behaviour. Amy tells her that Janis is coming out on the 3 May and that she can't wait for her friend to meet her mother.

However, just moments later, when Mitch makes an appearance, Amy asks him loudly, 'When is Mum coming

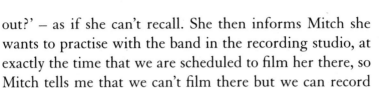

out?' – as if she can't recall. She then informs Mitch she wants to practise with the band in the recording studio, at exactly the time that we are scheduled to film her there, so Mitch tells me that we can't film there but we can record him instead by the pool.

Enough is enough!, I think. Mitch is obviously upset with Amy but he doesn't treat her like she is a 25-year-old woman, rather more like a five- or six-year-old child, and he doesn't tell her that her behaviour is unacceptable in this instance. So *I* tell Mitch that as we hadn't planned to film him again, and I don't see the point of taping Amy if she is being difficult and unpredictable, that 'filming is over'.

Mitch, looking as if he is about to explode, rushes off to the studio to confront his daughter. After about 30 minutes he comes back, extremely red faced, and says to me that it's all OK now and that we can film. 'Amy's expecting us …', he adds.

'Are you sure?' I ask.

With some trepidation, we head over to the studio with our TV crew and stills photographer. I am quite nervous, I have to admit, as I can't judge what will happen next. Mitch admits to me later on that, although he had strong words with Amy, he also wasn't sure what to expect!

As we head into the studio, Amy, who is still obviously drunk, rushes up to me and hugs me sweetly. The girl, who had previously appeared so hostile to me, less than hour ago, is now smiling. She dances for my TV camera crew and photographer. When she finally stops performing, she glances at Mitch and says to the other musicians, 'Let's put on that song.'

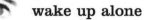

When the music starts again, Mitch's eyes become moist. He is almost crying. The song is 'Daddy's Home!'

Amy is now sitting on the drums, obviously drunk, but trying to play along to the tune. She nearly falls over.

Then she says, 'Dad, Dad, come here ...'

She motions to Mitch, and gives up her seat at the drums to him. When he starts playing, Amy picks up the guitar and plays with him. Then she runs to him and gives him a kiss full on the lips.

It is heartbreaking. Becoming sweet Amy, once again, she is trying so much to please him and she is so drunk. All I can think is, 'Wow! Why is she doing this to herself?'

Mitch is very emotional. Amy won't let us leave the studio before she's hugged me tightly. She tells me so politely: 'I *will* see you at the party. We are *all* coming!' She motions to her band. 'I am looking forward [to it]. When are you expecting us?'

☆ ☆ ☆

Later that day, we are at the barbecue by the pool and it is a relaxed atmosphere. Mitch has been talking about Amy's record and how he believes it will be out in September 2009. Some of the band members are already there and it is clear they don't share his optimism.

From time to time I hear him asking where Amy is. My producer tells him that he bumped into Amy outside Mitch's villa. She had told Erbil how happy she is about 'Daphne's party'! But Erbil thinks she seems frightened and insecure about when and how to come to the barbecue.

There is still no sign of Amy and although Mitch is trying hard to relax and enjoy himself, it is obvious that he can't. He is on edge. Suddenly we hear the clatter of high heels on stone and there is Amy, making what can only be described as a Hollywood entrance!

She is dressed, as usual, in a short dress, this time with one shoulder. Her hair has been put up elegantly. She looks very glamorous.

'Wow!' I tell her. 'Amy, you look beautiful!'

Amy looks really pleased by my comment. She says quietly, '*I did it for you.*'

Mitch tells me later that he has told Amy that she looks really well. 'It is important to give her compliments from time to time and build her confidence,' he adds.

Amy is still carrying the tarot cards with her and she begins to shuffle the pack. This brings us back to the subject of her grandmother, Cynthia. When I remark that Cynthia was a beautiful woman – Mitch showed me photographs and cine footage when we first met of Cynthia and I had then commented on how gorgeous his mother was – Amy says proudly: 'Listen! If Frank Sinatra [had] ever met my Nana Cynthia, Ava Gardner would *never* have had a chance with him!'

We talk about how Amy was so close to her grandmother and suddenly she begins to cry. Moments later, she is posing for the camera in a series of sexy positions, sitting first on one of the musician's laps, then her father's. After that, she perches on the laps of Mitch's friends.

Then she runs inside the villa and brings out her laptop to play some old, romantic songs to the guests. Amy tells us

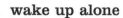

that after she married Blake, he chose the music. She imitates some of this and makes it clear that she doesn't think his taste is great. I sense that Amy is angry with her husband, perhaps because she still doesn't understand why he is divorcing her. I notice Mitch can't meet my eyes.

Later, Amy, who is drinking red wine (she has been drinking it all evening), decides that everyone should have ice cream. She insists on getting it from the fridge herself and also on serving it to us, tottering around the pool on the alarmingly high heels she is wearing. She watches me carefully to see if I'll eat the dessert.

While she is serving another guest, the inevitable happens: she trips and falls over, injuring herself. While we rush around, trying to find the first aid box, Amy is dismissive of the wound. She sits on Mitch's lap and murmurs, 'I don't want to spoil Daphne's party …' We put a plaster on it, all the same.

☆ ☆ ☆

It is very late. Mitch is scheduled to leave the island the next day but my team and I have another day here just to relax and unwind; even knowing this, I am so exhausted, I need to go to sleep.

Then the subject of Amy's forthcoming performance at the jazz festival on 8 May comes up. Amy suddenly remembers that we both love Hervé Léger and that I had told her earlier she could have one of my new dresses as a gift. She starts urging me to bring a couple of them over so she can try them on now. I tell her that it really is too late and that she can come to my villa tomorrow and pick one.

But Amy is on a mission: she must come to my villa NOW. Nothing else is acceptable.

Mitch is trying to intervene, but Amy won't be stopped. She has to get into my closet! She grabs my hand, holding it tightly, and drags me over to my place – my entourage, her entourage, all following ...

Mitch also tags along, shooting me apologetic looks as we enter my villa. Amy runs upstairs at an alarming pace to my bedroom, with me in tow. She is reverting back to her earlier behaviour and is becoming nasty, saying horrible things about her parents: 'People are trying to get through to me through my mother. My mother is handicapped and she is lonely.

'They will try to get me to sign papers. Each time my father is here people want me to sign papers.' I am surprised that even so boozed up she seems fairly astute. Mitch has brought people with him to the island to discuss Amy's business, but as of yet he hasn't accomplished anything. Amy obviously knows this. She understands more than people give her credit for.

She picks two of my Hervé Léger dresses: a purple one, which is short, but even more so when Amy rearranges it to suit her, and a black-and-white one, which is more elegant and which I hadn't expect her to pick. She tries on the purple one first, folding it up to her crotch. I tell her, 'Amy, I would leave it down ... otherwise you don't need to bother about a dress ...'.

She ignores me and instead keeps saying, 'My Daddy is always bringing people [here] for business. ... Why don't [these] people talk to *me*?'

She is now naked and she looks at me in what I guess is

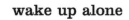

meant to be a seductive way, which would be funny as she is so drunk, but it is actually heartbreaking.

She continues, 'Daph, if people want to do business with me … they shouldn't go through my parents.'

She then repeats that people are taking advantage of her mother, who is lonely. Janis, Amy tells me, doesn't have a boyfriend! Amy says this to me as if it is the end of the world to be without a man.

At this point I could tell her that Mitch has said that Janis does have a new boyfriend – but it's none of my business. That's between them. But it's odd that Amy, who claims to be so protective of her mother, so close to her, doesn't know this.

Amy then begins to make hurtful remarks about both of her parents and I can sense an underlying violence in her behaviour.

I have had enough. It is not acceptable. I tell her, 'Amy does it ever occur to you that maybe the people who you claim are friends of your parents or who are talking to your parents are actually interested in [them] and not only you. You are not the most interesting person in the world. In fact you are becoming very boring. I don't want to hear all this.'

Amy is shocked. No one talks to her like this. She cries: 'What do you mean?! [Do] you know how famous I am?'

I say, 'Amy, … I am more known in some countries than you …'

Even drunk and naked, Amy is funny. She looks at me and says, 'Let's wrestle [to see] who is more famous!'

I tell her no. There's no point. I add that Amy can be

even more famous than she already is, if she just goes back to what she became famous for – her music, her talent – not the things for which she is now *infamous*.

My words strike a chord with Amy. She is quiet and then she murmurs finally, 'Why are you so sweet?' – before she starts to cry.

Then her mood changes. She asks me again if we can swap dresses and says, 'I am taking these two. I will give you two.'

Thanks but no thanks, I think. She can have one of them, as I promised, as a gift, but Amy is insistent: she must have both dresses.

'Amy, just take one dress and go to sleep,' I say.

But she refuses to listen to me. She is also becoming more aggressive. Mitch is trying to break in, seemingly to both protect me and to control his daughter, but Amy tells him that she doesn't want him and asks him to send in Neville, her bodyguard, to ask his opinion on the dresses. Neville enters the room, leaving Mitch and Amy's chief bodyguard, Andrew, outside.

Amy is naked and drunk when Neville comes in and he is obviously uncomfortable, not knowing where to look. I am tired by her behaviour; the evening is becoming increasingly more bizarre.

Amy repeats, 'I am taking both [dresses]' and Mitch and Andrew, who are now both in the bedroom, are trying to stop her.

I don't want this to explode into an even worse situation, so I say to her calmly but coldly, 'OK Amy. I am giving you one dress as a gift. You want to steal the second one? OK. Go ahead! Steal it … I am not going to report you to the police because your parents are my friends. I feel sorry for you. If it gives you … pleasure to steal a second dress, please – be my guest.'

The words seem to have the right effect. Amy changes instantly from being almost out of control to a little girl, who needs love and approval. She visibly melts, hugging me again and again, and crying, 'You are so sweet. You are so nice!'

Mitch steps in, telling Amy authoratively, 'Amy! [Daphne] is giving you a very expensive gift … one new dress … not two …!'

His words just seem to set Amy off again, however. She begins modelling both dresses, this time for her father, her bodyguards and me. She is in love with both of them. She can't let them go. The night has become far too long and I am tired.

Mitch looks apoplectic. He is trying to control his daughter but he can't.

Amy keeps repeating, 'Daphne, I love it,' as she tries on one dress after another. 'I love you. Let's swap dresses.'

Mitch cuts his daughter off, saying, 'You have to let Daphne and everyone else go to sleep. Daphne does not want your old dresses. [Just] pick one. It is very generous for Daphne to give [a dress] to you. Let's leave!'

But now Amy has a new urgent plan. She wants me to go to her villa, next door, to look at *her* dresses. This, she thinks, might convince me to change my mind about swapping the new dresses with two of her old ones. Since this is the only way to get her out of my home and enable the rest of my team to go to sleep, I let her drag me outside. Her worried father follows … as do my entourage; her entourage …

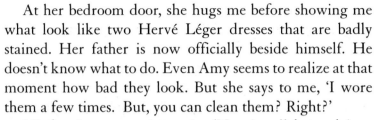

At her bedroom door, she hugs me before showing me what look like two Hervé Léger dresses that are badly stained. Her father is now officially beside himself. He doesn't know what to do. Even Amy seems to realize at that moment how bad they look. But she says to me, 'I wore them a few times. But, you can clean them? Right?'

Mitch tries to step in again. 'No, Amy!' he exclaims, 'She can't!'

But Amy isn't finished, looking through her wardrobe for another dress for me to try on. She produces a garment that looks like a Jewish bar mitzvah dress from the 1940s. It looks like it is made from a curtain and is probably a size 0.

She says, 'Daph, this is for you.'

I reply, 'Take one of the dresses I just gave you and let's go to sleep.'

Amy replies, 'I bought it for Mitch's wife, Jane, but she is too fat.'

Mitch overhears this and comments, '*Anybody* would be too fat for this dress. This dress is size 0.'

Amy ignores her Dad, saying to me, 'It would be wonderful on you.'

Mitch intervenes, 'Daphne doesn't want it.'

There is no point in explaining to her that I don't like to wear curtains and I don't need a new dress. Instead, I tell Mitch, 'Just let me show her it doesn't fit and that will be the end.'

I go to try it on and funnily enough it almost fits. Amy is jumping up and down in her excitement and she is screaming. She is trying to zip it up and is almost killing me in the process. She yells, 'Where are the bodyguards? They will zip it all the way up.'

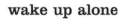

She is about to cut off my oxygen supply, hurting me, as long as I fit into the dress. I have really had enough.

'Look Amy,' I tell her. 'I am giving you a nice beautiful dress. I know you mean well. REALLY. Let's just go to sleep.'

Amy now wants me to stay with her alone and she cries when I tell her that I am leaving for America the next day. She asks me why I am going.

I say, 'Not because I don't love you. I have other work. I would love to stay with you.'

Suddenly, I felt sorry for her. She looks so lonely and sweet; so vulnerable. I hug her and tell her: 'Look, Amy, it is not about the dress. It doesn't matter if you wear this dress or anything else. You are going to be beautiful and walk on the stage and show them. If you are not ready, don't be afraid. Just tell your managers. … It is better to tell them you are not ready and let them make a statement [about it].'

Amy is very quiet but she is listening, although I am not at all sure that she understands what I am saying. She is still holding onto me and hugging me. I continue, 'If you do go there, whether in this dress or anything [else], just be beautiful and show them how good you are. Show them how big you are.'

She starts crying again and through her tears says, *'But Daph, I did show them. I did show them how good I am – five years ago.'*

I hug her closely because this is the moment of truth and I don't think any of the people around her are willing or able to deal with it. Amy doesn't think she can do it again. She doesn't believe that she can repeat her big successes of

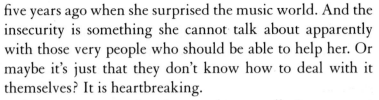
five years ago when she surprised the music world. And the insecurity is something she cannot talk about apparently with those very people who should be able to help her. Or maybe it's just that they don't know how to deal with it themselves? It is heartbreaking.

I carry on reassuring Amy and eventually I manage to bail out, making my escape. I give her a final supportive hug and, absolutely shattered, leave her to her equally exhausted father.

☆ ☆ ☆

Ten minutes later – it's about 4 a.m. – and Erbil, Steve and I are sitting on the first floor of our villa, shell-shocked by what we've just seen and experienced. We are all so tired that we just stare at each other and no one makes the move to go to our rooms on the second and third floors of the house.

Boom!

We jump as the door is flung open.

What now? I think.

It's Mitch. He hasn't rung or knocked to announce himself. He's just walked in. He looks like he's been through a war zone.

He doesn't even try to apologize to Erbil or Steve, who he knows well, just focuses on me and tells me urgently: 'Daphne! I need to speak to you alone.'

I don't have the energy to go upstairs for us to talk in private, so I open the door, which leads out to a small swimming pool, where there are some chairs and a table. We turn on the light and I look at Mitch. Frankly, I feel sorry for him; he looks as if all the energy has been sapped out of him.

After a few moments, he says, 'Daphne, I need you to do a favour for me. I need you to leave with me tomorrow.'

Well, that's unexpected! I think. And impossible! We are scheduled to stay one more day and we all need the time now, to rest and relax on the beach and think about our next assignment and forget about *Saving Amy* for a moment or two.

I ask him why I need to do this.

Mitch just repeats, '... You have to leave with me! I am so scared for your security. ...'

I reply, 'How can that be? ... I am not alone. I have all my people here with me and we all have tickets leaving Wednesday, not tomorrow, and I wouldn't leave them behind [anyway]. It is now 4 a.m. and my offices in New York and London are closed.'

Mitch doesn't even seem to hear this. He just looks extremely frightened.

'Daphne I am scared,' he admits. 'I am afraid to leave you here alone. ... my daughter ... you know ... it is not about the drugs and it isn't about Blake or all the alcohol that she drinks. My daughter is very sick. She has a psychiatric problem ... she needs to go for a very long treatment. ...

'I am scared to leave you here because she confuses you with me. She tries to please you all the time but then because of her problems with me she is getting violent and she [could become] violent with you.'

I don't think I have ever seen Mitch this truthful before. He really believes what he is saying. He doesn't meet my eyes, though, and instead looks at the table; he also seems to be talking more to himself than to me.

What he is saying is shocking. I try to be practical, all the while thinking, 'Well what does he want? How can I even get my team out of here in a few hours?'

I ask him to explain: 'What do you mean you are scared for me? I have Erbil here. I have Steve. I have your security and the hotel security. [Amy] cannot hurt me and frankly I don't think she [would]. ... Yes, she [has been] violent a few times, but not against me. It was more about you and Janis and all [her other] relationships.'

Mitch continues, 'I am very scared and if I leave you here without me things could get out of control and you are very important to me and I really wouldn't know what to do!'

At this point it is 4.30 a.m. and Mitch looks frightened, perhaps more from his own admissions to me. Possibly for the first time he has said out loud to someone, 'My daughter is sick. She has psychiatric problems.'

I am exhausted though. I tell him, 'Why don't you go and get some sleep and let me go and talk to everybody... .' I say to him that if we can't leave, maybe he should stay another day. 'We can change your ticket. I can chip in, it makes much more sense?'

He repeats something he has said to me before, 'No I can't. Jane will divorce me.' After which he leaves.

All I can think is: 'Wow'. Even after all that has happened this evening – his daughter's erratic behaviour, her performance over the dresses and Mitch's own belief that she might harm me, which led him to storm into my villa at 4 a.m. without any ceremony at all – Mitch's main concern is that his seemingly lovely wife, Jane,

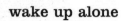

will divorce him if he stays one more day – even if he explains to her that he is worried about my well-being? It just doesn't make sense. All this serves to convince me further that the mission to 'save Amy' might just provide a good cover for so many other problems in this seemingly 'normal' family.

beat the point
to death

In the end, Erbil, Steve and I don't get to bed until 6 a.m. I am shocked by Mitch's revelations and we are also trying to see if we can possibly reschedule our flights. Despite all this, I have agreed to meet Mitch later that morning, around 10.30 a.m., in order to film at the bar Amy has been frequenting on the beach. A storm is brewing, so we postpone that, walking along the beach instead. We are all exhausted.

Mitch is behaving oddly, looking over his shoulder the whole time. 'Oh, I hope Amy is not up. Let's finish it before Amy gets up!' he says. After six days of bizarreness, I am annoyed and say, 'So what if she is up?! She knows that we are filming. She has been filming with us.'

The wind has picked up so much and is so noisy that it makes it impossible to hear each other, so one of the television crew tells us that we will have to film in one of our villas. Mitch's would be best because it is bigger than mine, but he refuses: 'No! What if Amy comes in?'

By this point, I want more than anything to vanish from the island and get some distance from Mitch for a while – instead, I put my foot down. 'So, what if [Amy] walks in? She knows about the filming. She is very smart. She talked to me about it last night. *So what?* What do you have to hide?'

We end up going to my villa, which is not very well situated, and film outside, even though it is not the best place and there is too much sunlight.

Mitch murmurs, 'Maybe I am part of [Amy's] problem.'

I remain quiet, even though he repeats it again.

☆ ☆ ☆

I ask Mitch how he feels about the recent events involving his daughter. He must be in a state of turmoil with so much to digest, I think, especially now he is going back to London.

'What is going on in your mind?' I say.

'In the first place I am glad to be going home to see my family. And knowing that Amy is safe and happy, that's good … but primarily I am glad to be going home,' he says.

'There is a lot to digest,' I tell him. '… [And] also there [must be] a lot of continuing worries, right?

'… Some of the people she speaks to … can hurt her?' I add.

'I don't know about that,' he says. 'I don't know about *hurt* her. If you mean by selling a story … I would not call that hurting her. I have to say … that's her business. If she wants to [talk to people] she is going to have to suffer the consequences. The consequences are not going to be great

[if] someone … sell[s] a story to one of the tabloids that she ran into the bar topless at dinner. I am just giving you an example – she never did *that*. [I have] different worries. They are not on the same magnitude as they were six months ago. What it shows is that we are returning to a kind of normality. … We have got an awful long way to go. … It is going to be a rocky road but we are certainly moving in the right direction, there is *no* question about it,' he says with conviction.

'I don't think people understand what you are going through,' I tell him. '… It is a terrible feeling to know that you are a parent of an adult, right, and in [Amy's] case, a very talented adult, and you still have to worry all the time. [It's] like you have a little baby [and] you don't know what will happen next.'

'I am glad that you brought that up because a lot of these things that are worrying me wouldn't be worrying me if I weren't here. I tend sometimes to make [a] situation worse than what it is … exacerbate [it] and make it much worse because in my mind [Amy] is not talking to a nice woman on the beach, she is talking to a potential drug dealer, [for example]. She is not … but unfortunately that is how my mind has been working.

'So,' he continues, 'what I have got to do is try and retrain my mind so that when I see her talking to a perfectly normal person on the beach, that is fine. I don't need to intervene. Why shouldn't she be … saying anything other than pleasantries? Sometimes I think I make the situation worse, unquestionably.'

'Just by being there?' I query.

'Not by being there,' he replies. 'But by my reaction …'

☆ ☆ ☆

'... [Amy] is not partying now,' Mitch says to me later. 'Now, she is getting down to work. She is getting back into her music.'

'[But] you [will] always have to worry about her,' I say to him. 'It is like you have a beautiful little baby and you have to run after her ... Does [it] cross your mind that you always have to be worried [about her]?'

'Yes,' Mitch says. '... All the time. But I worry about my son [Alex], too – and there is nothing to worry about with my son.

'I am a worrier. I can't help it.'

☆ ☆ ☆

We discuss the forthcoming festival at which Amy is going to make a much anticipated appearance.

'So what is Amy going to sing?' I ask.

'Frankly, I don't know. The band is not here yet. They are arriving only next week,' Mitch says. 'She is working with her producer Salaam [Remi] and the engineers [on] her new record.' He adds, 'As you saw Daphne, she has a very short attention span [so] they are recording everything she does. Then, they will select [material].

'So ... over the next couple of weeks, there isn't going to be as many gaps as there [have been] for her to fill,' he adds. 'I am not saying that she will not be able to go down to the beach and go horse riding – she probably will – but she is not going to be able to disappear for five to six hours. She is going to have to come back because everybody is on a tight

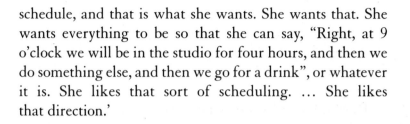

schedule, and that is what she wants. She wants that. She wants everything to be so that she can say, "Right, at 9 o'clock we will be in the studio for four hours, and then we do something else, and then we go for a drink", or whatever it is. She likes that sort of scheduling. ... She likes that direction.'

☆ ☆ ☆

'So, what is the story with Blake?' I say.

I had asked Mitch when I first arrived on the island why he thought Blake had been so quiet. At that time, Mitch was dismissive of his son-in-law, saying, 'Who cares about him? He has nothing to say?', which I took at the time to be denial, denial, denial. Blake is someone who, whether he is being good or bad, sells interviews to newspapers and he hadn't, at that point, really spoken to anyone since his release from jail. I told Mitch then, 'There is a newspaper out there, whether it is the *News of the World,* or the *Sun* or somebody else, who is [probably] paying him a lot of money to shut up [now] and they will come and interview him at the right time.'

But Mitch didn't like that. He didn't want to deal with that reality. And – a few months later – Blake gave an exclusive interview to *The Sun*.

But, of course, today, Mitch surprises me when I ask him about Blake as his attitude seems much more conciliatory. He says that Amy and Blake aren't in touch with each other, but adds, 'I can understand what she is going through and also what *he* is going through. They are two people who love each other. And have come to the realization that they cannot see each other. It will be dangerous for both of them. But I understand how difficult it must be, not to be able to see the person you are in love with.

'I am in love with Jane, my wife, and if I couldn't see her – it will be the most painful thing for me. Look, maybe one day – if they are both clean and strong enough – they can see each other. But for now – they both understand that it can't be.'

After the interview, I say to him in private that I'm surprised at his mellow attitude towards Blake. Mitch explains, 'I am upset and I miss Jane. I want to see Jane and I want to see my son. I want to be out of here.'

And that frankly makes two of us.

I feel bad for him because I know Mitch loves Jane and I know he means what he says. He feels helpless seeing Amy drinking but things are not going well and I feel so tired, watching Mitch lying to himself again.

☆ ☆ ☆

The reality of the situation is that despite Mitch's seemingly optimistic attitude towards his daughter, one which leads him constantly to be disappointed, there is no record on the horizon, as the London producer has already informed us. The musicians who have flown out to work with Amy are lovely but there isn't much going on creatively in Amy's studio. They are just hanging out there most of the time, although the studio is paying them.

Universal had sent out a lovely couple of executives to talk to Amy about her options since she hasn't released a record in years. She is a challenge for them as she hasn't performed recently and her last gigs were troubled, to say the least, but the couple are game. They bring out papers for her to sign via Mitch but, as Amy made clear the night before we left the island, she wants people to deal with her directly. And so, she decides not to deal with the people from Universal at all, even going so far as to insult the woman at my birthday meal. The two record executives are very nice people but they leave the island looking frustrated. They have taken a nine-hour flight, a three-hour cab journey and a helicopter ride to see Amy and work with her. They leave empty handed. This is Amyland.

☆ ☆ ☆

After we finish filming, Amy shows up later at my villa to say goodbye. Mitch is with her. She has on her trademark denim cutoffs and a bikini top. This morning's femme fatale is back to being a little girl. She hugs me again and again.

At one point, she sucks her thumb, which she has done before in my company. But this time Mitch, who is aware that a New York film crew is present, just pushes her thumb away – like you do with a small child. I suddenly have a flashback to yesterday's shoot – so, it's okay for Mitch to kiss his daughter on the lips, but not for Amy to suck her thumb in front of the cameras?

I repeat what I said to her in the early hours, before I left her villa. To make it big on the 8 May.

But now Amy is on the defence: 'I *AM* BIG!' she cries.

'Great,' I say, adding, 'Go and make everybody in the audience fall in love with you.'

'*But they are!*' Amy replies, immediately. '*Everybody is.* I *know* it. When [I] go on stage, I *feel* it.'

She hugs Erbil goodbye and he wishes Amy good luck, in turn, but she doesn't like this either and tells him, 'I don't *need* luck. ...'

As we leave, Amy says to me, 'Daphne, I love you. I really love you. I *really* love this girl ....'

We bump into Amy again, a little while later, outside. This time she is even sweeter. She hugs me again and says simply, 'Let me walk with you and wait for the car.'

☆ ☆ ☆

Just a few days later Janis flies to St Lucia, just before the jazz festival, to be with her daughter. She has her new boyfriend in tow. Mitch has already told me about him, when I commented on how lonely Janis seems. He says, 'Not any more', and proceeds to tell me that Janis has got together with one of his oldest friends over Passover. He says, 'Amy will have a fit. She has known him since she was a kid.'

I tell him, 'It is not Amy's life. It is Janis's life.'

When I ask if Amy knows, Mitch tells me that Janis is going to break it to Amy in May, just before the festival. Mitch is worried about how she will react to the news.

It is Janis's decision to come out and I ask Mitch if he thinks it's the right time. He says, 'Daphne, I don't know. Janis's relationship with Amy is very strange. I cannot tell Janis what to do and when to come.'

I can see the irritation in his face as he says this. Again, it is difficult to judge him because he has been living with the situation, even though he knows it will just add tension and stress to Amy, who is dealing with the expectation of her comeback. On the other hand he has to do something about it, surely? He is Amy's father. Why can't he just say to Janis: 'This is not a good time for you to come and to introduce your new boyfriend NOW! Amy is not as good as I am telling people. Why don't you do it after the gig?' Or, 'This is not the time for her to feel guilty that she doesn't have the time to spend with you. It will just put pressure on her.' But he doesn't.

And, for some reason, while Janis is able to talk to me and Amy is able to talk to me, these two people – mother and daughter – just can't communicate with each other in a warm, straightforward manner.

Don't get me wrong, they talk to each other – but they just don't express what they feel.

☆ ☆ ☆

After Amy goes on stage on the 8th, I receive countless messages on my phone saying it is her worst performance ever. I had seen it coming – anyone's dog could have seen it coming – but Mitch couldn't.

Before Amy went on stage I tell Mitch that Amy shouldn't perform, 'If you let her go on stage, the pictures will be worse than those of her crawling around like a horse.' Mitch has explained that the January photographs of Amy allegedly begging for alcohol on all fours were merely his daughter playing 'horse'.

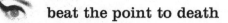

'Moreover,' I add, 'it will humiliate her and it will ruin her career for years.'

I am also thinking, why on earth, would you put your frightened daughter on that stage?

He informs me that Raye, Amy's manager, is over in St Lucia and that he's seen her and that everything is OK.

But Amy's manager is not you, I think. He's not Amy's father. Why, on earth, is Mitch letting a manager choose what's best for his own daughter?

On the day of the festival, Amy had reportedly started drinking at 11.00 a.m. Afterwards Mitch comments, '... *Now, it's alcohol.*'

some
unholy war

Amy flies back to Britain on 12 July 2009 to deal with her marriage and also to face charges of assault. She bursts into tears at Gatwick Airport as she comes through security. The final break from Blake comes on Thursday, 16 July 2009 at the High Court in London. Two years, one jail term, numerous rehab attempts and one front-page scandal after another and the Winehouse–Fielder-Civil union is officially history. Or is it?

I recall Mitch saying to me in London that it is difficult to know what kind of influence Blake has over Amy. 'He certainly has a power … but by Amy's own admission he is extremely manipulative and extremely controlling. So, he is able to influence her, … not only her but other people as well, … in ways that you and I can't imagine.'

I also remember being with Mitch in St Lucia, just before I flew back. We had had several discussions about Amy and Blake's possible divorce during our time together,

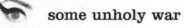

but this time, when it seems a likely event, I point out to Amy's father, '...They can live together even if they are divorced and frankly the forbidden fruit will smell [even] better [to] Amy.' Mitch agreed at the time, 'You are right. How do I prevent that?' The truth is that this is something that even control freak Mitch can't prevent. If these people are in love and are as co-dependent on each other as they appear, preventing them from seeing each other will just make their relationship all the more appealing.

Sure enough, within weeks of Amy and Blake's divorce, stories begin to surface about the couple's continued love for each other, with Blake reportedly declaring in the *News of the World* that he loves Amy as much as ever and that he knows 'she still loves me'. This is followed by other stories of 'secret flirting' on Facebook, alleged 36-hour love trysts and rumours that Amy and Blake will remarry in 2010.

☆ ☆ ☆

At the time of writing this, Amy is constantly in the press. Will she and Blake get back together? Are they getting married? Is she still on drugs? Is she still anorexic or bulimic? Will she ever produce another album? The attention and focus on Amy and her life is endless – from her latest hairstyle to her boob job. But, where does that leave Amy? What does the future hold for her? Does she still need saving? Or are her problems over?

Over the time I spent with Mitch, Janis, Jane and Amy, I learned a lot about their family and their relationship to 'saving Amy' and how it has impacted on the way they behave with each other. Sometimes, I feel, Amy's problems are used as an excuse to mask other underlying and undealt-with issues in the family. Certainly this seems to be the case in Mitch and Jane's relationship, among others.

In the end, I filmed 40 hours of sit-down interviews with regard to *Saving Amy*, and some of the events and conversations that took place are recorded in this book, but also during the time I spent with the Winehouses, we had several times more that in informal conversations. This allowed my crew and myself to learn lot about Amy and the family. There is, after all, nothing like those personal one-to-one conversations, when you are with someone in a relaxed environment, for allowing one to learn and understand the needs, fears, expectations and other emotions of the people who you are interviewing. Such conversations, over the years, have allowed me a much better understanding of my many celebrity interviewees – entertainers such as Michael Jackson and Liza Minnelli, heads of state such as Hillary Clinton and Nelson Mandela and actors such as Lauren Bacall and Mia Farrow.

One of the main things I learned about the Winehouses during that time is that they are not shy of talking to the press. Mitch, the man who informed me in one of our early meetings in London that he would talk about his private life, his family's private life 'only once', has spoken about it many times since.

I experienced this firsthand, shortly after we began filming the documentary. The French magazine *Closer* called to tell me that Janis and Mitch had already spoken to them via TF1, the leading national television station. I was surprised, but when I asked Mitch about it all he said was,

'Oh, but that was just before we met you. A few days before we met you.' It seemed odd but I didn't comment any further on his behaviour at the time. Then, the matter arose months later in March 2009, when Mitch was with my crew, Bitu and me at the Trader Vic's bar in London's Hilton Park Lane hotel. I had had a busy few months not just filming *Saving Amy*, but also working on my many other exclusives and for the several charities that I host. Mitch suddenly accused me of ignoring him and not paying him enough attention. The *Closer* and TF1 interviews came up during our subsequent conversation and I commented that none of my other interviewees, be it Michael Jackson's parents or Liza Minnelli, for example, had ever spoken to the press while I was interviewing them. *'I don't understand what we're doing anymore,'* I told him.

He denied having spoken to the magazine, saying he didn't even know who *Closer* was. He continued, 'You know Daphne, there are some satellites right now, I heard, that can just tape you from above and get what you're saying. *I never talked to anybody!'*

Mitch then mentioned that he had been approached by a company who wanted to film him interviewing the families of addicted people. He told me, 'I said "No. I'm doing things with Daphne."'

Now Mitch seems to be getting his 15 minutes of fame. As the *Guardian*, among other papers, commented in November 2009, *'Who will play the eponymous hero in 2015's most hotly anticipated biopic, The Mitch Winehouse Story?'*.

Once a London cabbie, it now seems the sky's the limit for Amy's Dad. The documentary he talked about subsequently aired as *My Daughter Amy* on Channel 4 in

January 2010, which led Amy to Tweet in response: '*Why don't my Dad WRITE a SONG when something bothers him instead of going on national tv? An you thought YOUR parents were embarrassing [sic].*'

Mitch has a chatshow and a reported record deal lined up – and he has even testified at a UK Home Affairs select committee hearing on the cocaine trade, about which he admitted he knew nothing.

And as Mitch himself has admitted, sometimes he makes situations worse through his actions or words. Certainly this seemed to be the case when he was asked about Amy's health on UK national television in October 2009. He replied 'fantastic, fantastic', but then added 'And her boobs are great as well', commenting on Amy's £35,000 breast enlargement job. Then he saw everyone's expressions, and added: 'I shouldn't have said that, should I? She looks absolutely fantastic'. He did, however, admit that Amy still has a long way to go in terms of her recovery.

'We're all recovering,' he stated.

This begs the question – *recovering from what?*

☆ ☆ ☆

So, after all this, what would be the best way to sum up how the Winehouses view Amy and her problems? Perhaps, it is best to leave you with something Mitch said to me during our many conversations:

'[Amy] is a wonderful person who only thinks about other people. ... so in that regard I think to myself I am the luckiest man in the world. Unfortunately, there is another aspect ... that she has a problem and in my family we have

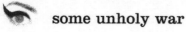

had situations like this – not with drugs but … when people have been sick – and the way we deal with [them] is not to shun them, not to move away from them but to move closer to them. Not smother them [but just] say "we are here for you" … "we love you" and "we will support you." And "if there is anything that we can do for you we are here.'"

This is apparently how the Winehouses see themselves 'Saving Amy'.

Above: Amy and Blake Fielder-Civil arriving at St Lucia
Hewanorra Airport to catch their flight back to the UK
after a holiday in September 2007.

Above: Mitch and Remi Nicole, Amy's friend and fellow singer-songwriter, bringing Amy's favourite KFC food to her in hospital in July 2008.

Opposite: Amy performing at the V Festival at Hylands Park, in Chelmsford, Essex in August 2008.

Above: Amy arriving at Westminster Magistrates' Court in London, on 24 July 2009, to face an assault charge.

Right: Amy with her old friend, Tyler James in Covent Garden, London, in September 2009.

Below: Amy performing with British band The Specials at the V Festival in Chelmsford, in August 2009.

Opposite: Mitch showing his support for his daughter by accompanying Amy to court in July 2009.

Above: Amy and Mitch in March 2009, when she impressed her father with her new-found appetite during lunch at a trendy London restaurant.

Above: Amy leaving her regular haunt, the Hawley Arms in Camden, London in November 2009.

notes

Will You Still Love Me Tomorrow?

1 Albert Gardens, near Commercial Road, London E1, in modern Tower Hamlets.
2 Charismatic leader of the British Union of Fascists (BUF), Sir Oswald Mosley led a march of his black shirt followers through Stepney, one of the largest Jewish communities in England at the time, on 4 October 1936, despite petitions to stop it as the black shirts had been terrorizing local Jews there for months. More than 250,000 east enders took to the streets to protest, resulting in the so-called Battle of Cable Street.
3 Classes to teach children about Judaism.
4 One of the leading performance art schools in London, named after its founder and principal Sylvia Young; former pupils include musician Emma Bunton (the Spice Girls).
5 Susi Earnshaw Theatre School in Barnet, North London.
6 Founded in 1959 by music maverick Chris Blackwell, Island Records quickly established itself as the label of choice with its diverse stable of artists. Its stable included everyone who was anyone in music – from Bob Marley, King Crimson, Jethro Tull, Nick Drake, Fairport Convention, Cat Stevens and Roxy Music to Robert Palmer, Grace Jones, U2, Pulp, PJ Harvey, DJ Shadow, Portishead, Free, Keane, Mika and Jack Johnson, to name but a few.

What Is It About Men

1 Tricky is an English rapper, musician and producer central to the trip-hop (a style of dance music, also known as the 'Bristol Sound' as it began there, played on electronic instruments and with a slow beat).

notes

2 Salaam Remi had worked with the best-selling band The Fugees and also with Nas, an influential American rapper who Amy had been listening to a lot at the time.

3 'Stronger Than Me' in the line 'Feel like a lady, but you my lady boy'.

4 Irving Berlin (1888–1989) was one of America's most influential composers.

You Know I'm No Good

1 Singer, actor and performer Charlotte Church hosts a self-titled show on Britain's Channel 4, featuring sketches, live performances from guests and by herself and also interviews with celebrities, such as Amy Winehouse.

Alcoholic Logic

1 'Help Yourself', *Frank* – 'I can't help you if you won't help yourself; I can't help you, if you don't help yourself'.

discography

Album releases [title, release date, record company]

Frank 20/10/2003 Island Records

Back To Black 13/03/2007 Island Records

Back To Black (deluxe edition – bonus disc) 12/11/2007 Island Records

Frank (deluxe edition – bonus disc) 15/05/2008 Universal

DVD

I Told You I Was Trouble 06/10/2008 Island Records

Singles

2003
'Stronger than me'   UK chart 71
'Take the Box'   UK chart 57

2004
'In my Bed/You Sent me Flying' UK chart 60
'Fuck Me Pumps/Help Yourself' UK chart 65

2006
'Rehab'   UK chart 7/US chart 9

discography

'You Know I'm No Good'   UK chart 18/US 77
'Back to Black'   UK chart 25
'Tears Dry on Their Own'   UK chart 16
'Love Is A Losing Game'   UK chart 46

As a featured artist [song, album, artist, chart position]

2007
'Valerie' (*Versions*, Mark Ronson) UK chart 2
'B Boy Baby' (Mutya Buena)   UK chart 73

Other featured appearances [song, artist, album]

2004
'Will You Still Love Me Tomorrow?', Soundtrack, *Bridget Jones: The Edge of Reason*

2005
'Best For Me', Tyler James, *The Unlikely Lad*

2006
'You Know I'm No Good' [remix], Ghostface Killah, *More Fish*

2007
'Cupid', *Radio 1 Established 1967*

2008
'Fools Gold', *Sex and the City:Vol 2, More Music*

2009
'Classics', *Rhythms Del Mundo*

picture
credits

PLATE SECTION 1

1. Amy Winehouse with butterfly hair accessory © G6010C/
   EMPICS Entertainment
2. Amy at HMV, Oxford Street in January 2004 © EMPICS
   Entertainment
3. Amy at the Mercury Music Prize ceremony in September 2004 ©
   Andy Butterton/PA Archive/Press Association Images
4. Amy with her award at the Mercury Music Prize ceremony in
   September 2004 © Getty Images
5. Amy at the BRIT awards in February 2007 © FilmMagic
6. Amy performing with Mick Jagger at the Isle of Wight Festival
   in June 2007 © Getty Images
7. Amy performing with Mark Ronson at the BRIT Awards in
   2008 © Alessia Pierdomenico/Reuters/Corbis
8. Amy with Blake Fielder-Civil at the 2007 MTV Awards in Los
   Angeles © Frank Trapper/Corbis
9. Amy Winehouse in orange dress © WireImage

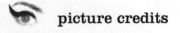 **picture credits**

PLATE SECTION 2

1. Amy in yellow patterned dress © Daphne Barak Photo Agency/Stephen Schwartz
2. Daphne with Janis and Mitch Winehouse at Les Ambassadeurs club in December 2008 © Daphne Barak Photo Agency/Erbil Gunasti
3. Daphne with Mitch and Amy Winehouse © Daphne Barak Photo Agency/Erbil Gunasti
4. Amy in St Lucia, April 2009 © Daphne Barak Photo Agency/Stephen Schwartz
5. Daphne with Mitch on Daphne's last night in St Lucia, April 2009 © Daphne Barak Photo Agency/Erbil Gunasti
6. Daphne with Mitch on Daphne's last night in St Lucia, April 2009 © Daphne Barak Photo Agency/Erbil Gunasti
7. Amy in St Lucia in pink dress © Daphne Barak Photo Agency/Erbil Gunasti
8. Daphne with Amy in St Lucia, April 2009 © Daphne Barak Photo Agency/Erbil Gunasti
9. Amy playing the guitar in her studio in St Lucia © Daphne Barak Photo Agency/Erbil Gunasti
10. Amy playing the guitar in her studio in St Lucia © Daphne Barak Photo Agency/Erbil Gunasti
11. Amy hugging her mother Janis after winning 5 Grammy awards © Getty Images for NARAS

PLATE SECTION 3

1. Amy with Blake Fielder-Civil at St Lucia Hewanorra Airport in September 2007 © Cruisepictures/EMPICS Entertainment

picture credits

2. Amy performing at the V Festival at Hylands Park, Essex in August 2008 © Suzan/EMPICS Entertainment
3. Mitch Winehouse with Remi Nicol, bringing Amy's favourite KFC food to her in hospital in July 2008 © Errol Griffith/ EMPICS Entertainment
4. Amy arriving at Westminster Magistrates' Court in London, on 24 July 2009 © Kirsty Wigglesworth/AP/Press Association Images
5. Amy with Tyler James in Covent Garden, London, in September 2009 © Fiona Hanson/PA Wire/Press Association Images
6. Amy performing with The Specials at the V Festival in August 2009 © Joel Ryan/AP/Press Association Images
7. Mitch Winehouse accompanying Amy to court in July 2009 © Samir Hussein/EMPICS Entertainment
8. Amy and Mitch in London, in March 2009 © Dominic Lipinski /PA Wire/Press Association Images
9. Amy leaving the Hawley Arms in Camden, London in November 2009 © Chicago/EMPICS Entertainment

acknowledgements

This book would have never happened without the support and contribution of the following people:

Erbil Gunasti, Bitu Bhalla, Terri Pace, Carol Ng, Stephan Schwartz, Vincenzo Liguri and Bob Scott.

I would also like to thank:

Hassiakos Sotiros of Les Ambassadeurs Club, London
Azad Cola, 'Stass' Zelijko Stasevic and Ashley Shaw of The
   Westbury, London
Simon Scoot of Intercontinental Park Lane, London
Reto Stockenius, Nicholas Labhart and Beniamino Poserina of
   Villa Sassa, Lugano, Switzerland
Kevin Snaggs of Cotton Bay Village, St Lucia